D0119006

Cutting Edge
Energy
Technology

ReferencePoint
Press®

San Diego, CA

Other books in the *Cutting Edge Technology* series

Cutting Edge Entertainment Technology
Cutting Edge Internet Technology
Cutting Edge Medical Technology
Cutting Edge Military Technology
Cutting Edge Transportation Technology

Cutting Edge Energy Technology

Stuart A. Kallen

ReferencePoint
Press®

San Diego, CA

For more information, contact:
ReferencePoint Press, Inc.
PO Box 27779
San Diego, CA 92198
www.ReferencePointPress.com

LIBRARY OF CONGRESS CATALOGING-IN-PUBLICATION DATA

Name: Kallen, Stuart A., 1955- author.
Title: Cutting edge energy technology / by Stuart A. Kallen.
Description: San Diego, CA : ReferencePoint Press, Inc., [2017] | Series: Cutting edge technology | Audience: Grades 9 to 12. | Includes bibliographical references.
Identifiers: LCCN 2015048422 (print) | LCCN 2015050356 (ebook) | ISBN 9781682820384 (hardback) | ISBN 9781682820391 (epub)
Subjects: LCSH: Power resources--Juvenile literature. | Energy development--Environmental aspects--Juvenile literature. | Technological innovations--Juvenile literature. | Renewable energy sources--Juvenile literature.
Classification: LCC TJ163.23 .K35 2017 (print) | LCC TJ163.23 (ebook) | DDC 621.042--dc23
LC record available at http://lccn.loc.gov/2015048422

Contents

Innovations in Energy Technology   6

Introduction   8
New Ideas for Old Problems

Chapter One   11
Next-Generation Renewable Energy

Chapter Two   23
Battery Breakthroughs

Chapter Three   35
Microbe Power

Chapter Four   47
Green Buildings

Chapter Five   59
The Internet of Things

Source Notes   70

For Further Research   73

Index   75

Picture Credits   79

About the Author   80

Innovations in Energy Technology

1831
British scientist Michael Faraday discovers the principle of electromagnetic induction using magnets and a loop of copper wire.

2001
In Taos, New Mexico, architect Michael E. Reynolds builds his first energy-efficient Earthship homes from recycled materials.

1999
The term *Internet of Things* is coined by British tech pioneer Kevin Ashton.

1954
Bell Laboratories creates the first photovoltaic solar cell to convert sunlight into electricity.

1800   1900   •••   1990   2000

1928
The theory of antimatter is put forth by English physicist Paul Dirac.

1998
The Canadian government legalizes the commercial growth of industrial hemp, a source of fiber used in bioenergy production.

1991
The first commercially available lithium-ion battery is marketed by Sony.

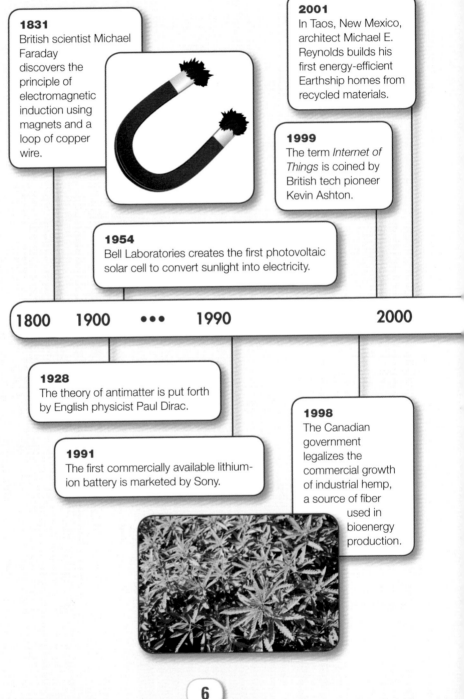

2003
The world's first wave-energy generation plant opens near Orkney, Scotland.

2014
Researchers in Shanghai, China, create a lithium-ion battery within yarn that can be weaved into textiles.

2009
Wind energy provides 2 percent of the total global electricity usage.

2013
The first large-scale commercial anaerobic digestion facility in the United States opens in San Jose, California.

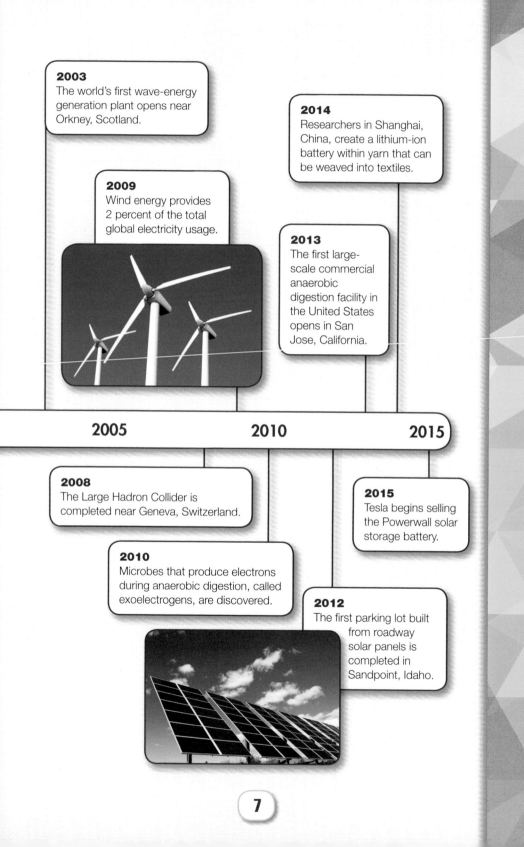

2005   2010   2015

2008
The Large Hadron Collider is completed near Geneva, Switzerland.

2015
Tesla begins selling the Powerwall solar storage battery.

2010
Microbes that produce electrons during anaerobic digestion, called exoelectrogens, are discovered.

2012
The first parking lot built from roadway solar panels is completed in Sandpoint, Idaho.

New Ideas for Old Problems

The United States had about 123 million households in 2015. Of that number, a tiny fraction—around 250,000—was estimated to be off the grid. These homes did not get their electricity from the nationwide system of interconnected power plants, transformers, and high-voltage lines known as the power grid. Those living off the grid use solar panels, windmills, and other methods to light, cool, and heat their homes.

If businessman Elon Musk has his way, the number of people living off the grid will continue to grow every year. Musk is an inventor and engineer and the founder of several companies, including the electric car company Tesla Motors and the solar energy firm SolarCity. In 2015 Tesla began manufacturing a rechargeable solar storage battery (SSB) called the Powerwall. The Powerwall is designed to accept a charge from solar panels during the day to provide all the power a homeowner needs at night.

Musk has brought a lot of media attention to SSBs. However, they are just one of dozens of cutting edge technologies under development that are focused on making better use of resources and energy. Some, such as producing power from rotting food and animal waste, are older technologies that are being updated for the twenty-first century. Other concepts, like obtaining energy from antimatter, remain the stuff of science fiction. But every idea is on the table when it comes to next-generation energy technology. And there is little doubt that future generations will receive their power in ways barely imagined by scientists, researchers, and inventors working today.

Slowing Climate Change

Many alternative energy researchers are driven by environmental concerns. They are searching for ways to reduce demand for coal and natural gas—the fossil fuels commonly used to generate

Solar panels like the ones on the roof of the house shown here generate electricity using energy from the sun. A relatively recent invention known as a solar storage battery collects energy from the panels during the day and powers the house at night.

electricity. The combustion of fossil fuels produces carbon dioxide (CO_2) emissions. Rising levels of CO_2 and other heat-trapping gases in the atmosphere have warmed the earth, leading to a phenomenon known as climate change. The wide-ranging impacts of climate change, scientists say, include rising sea levels; melting snow and ice; more extreme heat events, fires, and drought; and more extreme storms, rainfall, and floods.

Microsoft founder Bill Gates is one of many people around the globe who believe that humanity must develop alternate forms of energy to slow climate change. Gates wants to see more money invested in basic energy research and development and is willing to use some of his vast wealth for that purpose. He does not think the renewable energy technologies currently in use will do enough to reduce CO_2 emissions: "The only way you can get to the very positive scenario is by great innovation. Innovation really does bend the curve [toward stopping climate change]."[1] In 2015 Gates backed his words with the promise to invest $2 billion in green technology research and development over the next five years.

> **power grid**
>
> A coordinated network of power lines, transformers, and other equipment used to generate and distribute electricity over a wide area.

While Gates raises awareness about climate change, he understands that betting on any new energy technology is risky. Oil, natural gas, and coal are cheap and plentiful. Fossil fuels may be dirty energy sources, but most people cannot afford to buy expensive solar panels or a $3,000 household Powerwall battery.

Any new energy systems will need to work reliably when the sun is not shining and the wind is not blowing. As Gates points out, "Power is about reliability. We need to get something that works reliably."[2] And the modern energy grid is very reliable. It was developed and built over a period of more than a hundred years. Replacing major elements of the grid will require commitments from industry, government, and everyday power users. But anyone looking at the development of computers and the Internet since the 1980s can see that radical changes can happen quickly with the right technology.

Developments are taking place in research centers across the world that might transform the energy outlook in a matter of a few decades. While no one expects the transition to green energy to be cheap and easy, changes are already taking place and the future is coming soon to power outlets across the globe.

CHAPTER ONE

Next-Generation Renewable Energy

The twenty-first century has seen a rapid expansion in the use of renewable energy sources like solar and wind power. But researchers are looking beyond the sun and wind to harvest other sources of renewable energy from the environment. Some are squeezing power from sources like human footsteps and bike pedals. Others are diving underwater to harvest power from waves. Scientists are also thinking of the possibilities of renewable energy when they use the most sophisticated equipment on Earth to create antimatter, a substance that creates energy when atomic molecules crash into each other at high speeds. Scientist José Luis Cordeiro explains the importance of advancing new energy ideas: "Technological development [will open] the door to continuous and rapid worldwide economic growth and [allow] the world to achieve energy sustainability using many different energy sources."[3]

These energy research projects are part of a global push to reduce emissions of CO_2, one of the greenhouse gases responsible for climate change. Researchers hope these emissions—produced by the burning of coal, oil, and natural gas—will greatly reduce when the next generation of renewable energy sources comes online.

Pedal Power

Some of the sustainable energy sources attracting attention in the twenty-first century are based on kinetic energy, or energy produced by motion. Kinetic energy is produced by numerous sources, including the movement of wind, waves, and even molecules. One of the most basic ways to generate kinetic energy involves harnessing one of the oldest power sources—human muscles. People generate kinetic energy when they walk, run, or pedal a bicycle.

Scientists understand that the human body contains a huge

quantity of energy; the energy stored in the body fat of an average adult is equal to a 1-ton (.9 metric ton) battery. Humans expend this energy while performing everyday activities and replenish energy supplies by eating food. But kinetic energy can also be used to produce electricity. That idea is driving research on a new array of human-powered generators.

One of the best places to harness human energy is at a gym where people expend their energy on stationary bikes and elliptical trainers. Most bikes and trainers at gyms use electricity to power timers and monitors that tell people how fast they are moving and how many calories they are burning. But at the Green Microgym in Portland, Oregon, the bikes are not plugged into the power grid; instead, they harvest the kinetic energy produced when people cycle during their workouts.

kinetic

Caused by or pertaining to motion.

The Green Microgym uses 85 percent less power than a traditional fitness center. The exercise equipment at the gym has been modified to generate what is called micropower. On each stationary bike the rotating pedals power an electrical generator—a coil of copper wire that spins within a circle of magnets to generate electricity. The power generated by the pedals is then sent to the building's electrical grid to run equipment monitors, computers, lights, and other electrical devices. Excess power charges storage batteries, which keep the gym's lights on during times when fewer people are adding power to the grid with their workout routines.

A person riding a stationary bike equipped with a generator can produce about one hundred watts of electricity an hour. This is enough power to light a twenty-watt compact fluorescent bulb for about five hours. While the workout routine of one person would not do much to keep the lights on, dozens of people pass through a typical gym every day. Green Microgym owner Adam Boesel explains the concept:

> You don't need a ton of energy-sucking machines to get a good workout. We are machines. You power your workout.

Adam Boesel (left) and Andrew Wiley pedal stationary bicycles at Boesel's Green Microgym in Portland, Oregon. Because the exercise equipment in the gym is connected to the facility's electrical grid, using it produces energy to power lights, computers, and other devices that run on electricity.

The energy bar one member just ate powers the ceiling fan for the next three hours. Another member's morning scramble is doing its part to keep the lights on. Every revolution on the elliptical is churning pure electricity back to the grid. Calories are converted into precious watts.[4]

Harvesting Footsteps

While the Green Microgym can power its own operations, electricity can also be produced on a much larger scale by the kinetic energy of people walking down the street. That is the concept behind the London-based company Pavegen, which makes energy-producing floor tiles. Pavegen founder Laurence Kemball-Cook developed a tile that flexes about .2 inches (5 mm) when stepped on. The give and take, or flexing of the tile, produces

The Bicycle Desk

Doctors say it is unhealthy to sit at a desk all day and get no exercise. Likewise, environmentalists believe that using fossil fuel electricity to power computers and other devices is unhealthy for the planet. A small start-up company called Pedal Power in Essex, New York, believes its invention can improve the health of the climate—and the deskbound—at the same time.

Pedal Power's bike desk combines a chair, a desktop with electrical outlets, and a set of pedals attached to a generator. Users pedal while they work, and the generator powers the computers, cell phone chargers, and other electronic devices plugged into the desktop. In addition, the bike desk can perform other tasks with the pulley system attached to the pedals. For instance, farmers in rural India are using the pedal-powered desk to pump water for irrigation. Pedal Power cofounder Steve Blood explains how his invention could slow climate change while changing attitudes: "I would love to see Pedal Power machines in every coffee shop in every city in the country. So that people who are working on their laptops, working on their iPads, are at the same time generating their own power for those devices. I want to connect people to the energy they use. I want people to understand how precious energy is, and how hard it is to come by."

Quoted in James Hamblin, "The Electricity-Generating Bicycle Desk That Would Power the World," *Atlantic*, January 7, 2014. www.theatlantic.com.

kinetic motion that transforms into about six watts of electricity per footstep. For business reasons, Kemball-Cook will not reveal the precise details of how the tiles work. However, there is little doubt that the tiles are effective energy producers.

During the London Olympics in 2012, Pavegen installed tiles on the walkway leading to Olympic Park. About 1 million people used the tiled path, which generated twenty kilowatt-hours of energy. That was enough to light the street lamps next to the walkway at full power every night during the seventeen-day event. In addition, the tiles produced extra energy that went to London's electrical grid.

Harnessing a Wasted Resource

Pavegen tiles are powering up some of the busiest areas of London. Fifty-one tiles power the LED lights in a busy corridor at Terminal 3 at Heathrow Airport, generating electricity from more than 18 million people who pass through the terminal every year. Tiles can also be found powering LED lights at Harrods department store, the third most-visited sight in London, which attracts 15 million visitors a year.

In the United States, Pavegen tiles caught the attention of students in an advanced placement environmental science class at Bloomington High School South in Indiana. The students launched a project to have Pavegen tiles installed in the school's main entrance. The eight tiles only power a signboard and phone charging station, but students are hoping to line the hallways of the school with the tiles. This would provide enough power to keep the lights on at school all day, every day.

Power-generating tiles also light up one of the poorest neighborhoods of Rio de Janeiro, Brazil. The energy company Shell partnered with Pavegen to donate two hundred tiles for a soccer field in the Morro da Mineira neighborhood, where electrical service is sporadic or nonexistent. A typical soccer player runs about 7 miles (11 km) in a single game, and in Morro da Mineira, the players power the field lights with every step. Extra power lights neighborhood homes for up to ten hours after a game. This makes the people-powered soccer field the first of its kind in the world.

Although the Pavegen tiles remain expensive, the company hopes to bring their cost down to the same price as normal flooring. If that can happen, future families might power their homes by walking from the living room to the kitchen, bedrooms, and garage. The tiles could also be incorporated into the sidewalks in every city. As Kemball-Cook explains, "Human footfall is currently a wasted resource. We will become part of the fabric of urban infrastructure."[5]

infrastructure

Structures and facilities, such as roads, water and sewer lines, and power plants, needed for the operation of a society.

This people-powered soccer field in Rio de Janeiro, Brazil, is the first of its kind in the world. Thanks to special tiles, each step the soccer players take produces energy—enough to illuminate the field during the game and the surrounding neighborhood for about ten hours afterward.

Air Power

Human footsteps are not the only wasted resource scientists are trying to turn into electricity. Power plants produce excess energy during off-peak hours—late at night and early in the morning. The power plants do not shut down but continue to run at low levels while there is little demand for electricity.

Scientists are hoping to capture off-peak power plant energy with technology called compressed air energy storage (CAES). Compressed air technology takes excess electricity produced at off-peak hours and uses it to run air compressors. The compressors pump air into a vessel, where it is stored under extremely high pressure. When the demand for electricity increases, the pressurized air releases in a controlled manner, spinning a generator to create electricity. The off-peak energy produced by wind turbines and solar power stations can also work with a CAES system.

Electricity produced through CAES is very inexpensive. The compressed air can be stored in pipes or in naturally occurring caverns and underground caves. A company called LightSail has developed strong, lightweight carbon-fiber tanks to store compressed air. These tanks are being used in pilot programs at two renewable energy facilities, a solar power station in Ventura County, California, and a wind farm in Nova Scotia, Canada.

The Energy in Waves

Another form of cutting edge renewable energy can be found in the endless crashing of ocean waves on a beach. Wave energy is produced by the movement of the ocean and the changing heights and speed of the swells. And there is little doubt that the kinetic energy in waves is enormous. A single 4-foot (1.2 m) wave crashing on 1 mile (1.6 km) of coastline contains energy equal to the amount produced by twenty-six average wind turbines. However, harvesting that energy remains an elusive goal; the ocean environment is hostile and unpredictable.

Salt water is highly corrosive and damaging to sensitive machinery. This makes building anything in the ocean an expensive proposition. A facility built to capture wave energy, called a wave farm, could cost anywhere from $50 million to $100 million. Another problem with wave energy concerns the unpredictable movement of the ocean. Waves rise and fall, churn from side to side, and roll forward and backward. Waves can be small on a warm summer day or large and destructive during a storm. The unpredictability of waves and the financial challenges have caused numerous projects to fail in the quest to harness wave power.

Despite the challenges, researchers are working to build and install a new generation of wave-energy converters. The technology falls into two broad categories: wave generators that are submerged underwater and those that float on the surface. A pilot wave farm near Perth, Australia, is an example of an underwater installation. The company Carnegie Wave Energy has developed what it calls CETO wave-energy technology, which converts ocean swells into renewable power. (The name was inspired by Ceto, the Greek sea goddess.)

A CETO installation consists of several submerged buoys filled with air. The buoys attach to pumps fitted into a pipe on the seabed. The movement of the waves makes the buoys bob up and down. This action pumps seawater to shore under high pressure. The pressurized water turns an onshore generator that produces electricity.

In February 2015 a CETO installation in western Australia became the world's first operating wave power station. The $100 million project took ten years to complete and now provides renewable energy to Australia's largest naval base, the HMAS Stirling on Garden Island near Perth. The wave farm produces enough energy to power around eighteen hundred typical homes. On the base, it provides electricity for military housing, offices, a hospital, fueling stations, and two dozen ships berthed at the docks.

The cost of the CETO project demonstrates the shortcomings of wave power. Whereas a typical natural gas power plant costs ten times more—$1 billion—a gas plant powers one hundred times as many homes as a CETO installation. But as Carnegie Wave Energy CEO Michael Ottaviano points out, "The challenge from here on is really about scale and cost. We need to make the technology bigger, we need to make our projects bigger because that's what allows you to get your costs down."[6] Ottaviano envisions a future when a single large wave farm will produce the same amount of power as a modern natural gas plant for the same price.

buoy

An anchored nautical device that carries signals or shows the location of reefs and other hazards.

Antimatter Energy

Although wave energy might someday power coastal cities, a substance created by physicists might one day power everything from electricity plants to spaceships. The substance is antimatter, and it is perhaps the most futuristic renewable energy source ever conceived.

To understand antimatter, it is necessary to recognize that everything in the universe is made of atoms called matter. Each atom of matter contains particles called protons, electrons, and neutrons. Matter makes up the substance of all objects with mass and volume. That includes all the planets and stars in the universe. Everyday objects made of matter include anything that can be touched, squeezed, or bumped into. In technical terms, matter exists in four states: solid, liquid, gas, and plasma. (Plasma is found in lightning and electric sparks.)

The theory of antimatter was put forth in 1928 by English physicist Paul Dirac. He stated that every particle of matter has another particle of antimatter that is its mirror opposite; antimatter

Buoy Power

Capturing the power of unpredictable ocean waves is extremely difficult, and dozens of test projects have failed to produce significant results. The backers of a test project in Oahu, Hawaii, are defying the odds by producing electricity from the kinetic energy of the ocean.

In 2015 a company called Northwest Energy Innovations partnered with the US Navy, the US Department of Energy, and the University of Hawaii to create a 45-ton (41 metric tons) buoy called Azura. The device is the first of its kind to produce electricity from 360 degrees of motion; it captures both the heave (up-and-down) and surge (side-to-side) motions of the waves. The kinetic energy of the Azura transfers to a rotating generator mechanism beneath the water, and the power is sent to the electrical grid through an underwater cable.

During a twelve-month test period at the US Navy Wave Energy Test Site near Oahu, the Azura produced about twenty kilowatts of electricity. This is a weak output for such a huge device—only enough to power two or three homes. However, researchers hope to develop a similar-sized buoy that will one day produce enough electricity for one thousand homes. Thousands of these wave-power buoys could be placed in ocean waters around the country and potentially provide half of all electricity used in the United States.

particles have the same mass but opposite electrical charges. For example, for each electron there is an antielectron. When a particle of matter collides with a particle of antimatter, the particles destroy each other. They disappear into a powerful flash of pure energy. If this energy could be contained, it could be used to create steam to drive generators in an antimatter power plant.

Colliding Particles

Antimatter is the most potent power source known to humanity, and some of its theoretical uses sound like science fiction. Antimatter has been considered for use in weapons that would be many times more powerful than hydrogen bombs. And researchers have even considered using antimatter to power rocket engines. According to NASA, a tiny amount of antimatter—ten milligrams—would be enough for a round-trip spaceflight to Mars. Physicists also believe that the power of antimatter could be used for generating electricity, but this remains, at least for now, only a possibility.

Many obstacles would need to be overcome. The biggest problem is that antimatter does not exist in nature. It must be created atom by atom in a process that is enormously time-consuming and expensive. The only place antimatter has been made is in a facility known as the Large Hadron Collider (LHC) located in Geneva, Switzerland. The LHC, sometimes called a particle collider, was built between 1998 and 2008 by the European Organization for Nuclear Research. The LHC sits in a circular, 17-mile-long (27 km) tunnel located 547 feet (175 m) beneath the ground. It is the largest and most complicated single piece of machinery ever built.

The collider produces beams of charged particles consisting of protons and electrons. The particles propel through a circular beam pipe that runs the length of the LHC tunnel. Two beams traveling in opposite directions can be collided into one another. When this happens the collision produces small amounts of antimatter.

What's the Matter with Antimatter?

Over the course of a year, the LHC only creates a few trillionths of a gram of antimatter. This is enough to power a one-hundred-watt light bulb for just a few seconds. Because of the time and expense required to make antimatter, it is the most expensive substance on Earth. If it were possible to create a gram of antimatter, it would be worth an estimated $80 trillion. By comparison, the entire budget of the US government in 2015 was around $4 trillion.

Even if a gram could be made, there is no way to store more than a few atoms of antimatter. Nonetheless, advances in antimatter storage and production technology might someday make antimatter particle power stations possible. Researchers believe that if the price of antimatter could decrease to $1.5 million a gram, such stations could produce power at the same price as coal or natural gas. But even the most optimistic scientists do not believe this will happen before the end of the twenty-first century.

Another solution to obtaining elusive antimatter might involve traveling the far reaches of outer space. Physicists theorize that antimatter comets exist in the universe. If astronaut-miners could harvest .75 pounds (.45 kg) of antimatter from a comet, it would produce the energy equivalent of 1 million tons (907,185 metric tons) of coal. A ton of mined antimatter could provide all of the world's electricity for one year.

As long as humanity wants to keep the lights on without over-heating the planet, physicists will experiment with antimatter. Although it is an expensive and futuristic method for producing renewable energy, it is one tool among many intended to move the world away from fossil fuels. From the simplest machines to the most complex, there are limitless possibilities at the cutting edge of renewable energy research.

CHAPTER TWO

Battery Breakthroughs

Every year around 5 billion lithium-ion (li-ion) batteries are sold around the world. The ubiquitous batteries, which store a lot of power in a lightweight, compact form, are found in almost every portable electronic device, including cell phones, laptops, fitness trackers, hoverboards, and cameras. Li-ion batteries also power electric cars, unmanned aerial vehicles, robots, and the International Space Station. Sony introduced the first li-ion batteries to consumers in 1991. Since that time the various devices that use the batteries have transformed society, yet the design of the batteries has changed little in the past two decades.

Scientists are searching for ways to make batteries that cost less, charge faster, last longer, and are better for the environment. Better batteries will lower the cost of electric cars while giving them greater range. More efficient batteries will also be used to store power generated by solar panels and wind turbines for use when the sun is not shining and the wind is not blowing. Chemistry professor Clare Grey explains the push to develop the next generation of batteries: "Many of the technologies we use every day have been getting smaller, faster and cheaper each year—with the notable exception of batteries. . . . The challenges associated with making a better battery are holding back the widespread adoption of two major clean technologies: electric cars and grid-scale storage for solar power."[7] Some hope to bring about these changes by improving li-ion batteries, but others are looking to new materials and cutting edge technology to completely remake batteries.

Li-Ion Battery Problems

Researchers wishing to improve batteries have to work with three basic elements that generate electricity in all batteries, including li-ions. Batteries store and release energy by moving electrons between two posts called electrodes. One electrode is called the anode; the other is called the cathode. The third battery ingredient, located between the electrodes, is the electrolyte. In li-ion batteries, the electrolyte contains a salt solution with particles, or ions, of the silver-white metal lithium. When a li-ion battery is charged, lithium ions in the electrolyte are driven to the cathode. As the ions move, they flow through the electronic device that contains the battery, providing power. The concept is similar to a waterwheel turned by the falling water of a stream. But instead of flowing water, li-ion batteries work with steadily moving electrons.

The three main elements in li-ion batteries have flaws that researchers want to eliminate. One of the biggest problems with li-ion batteries is that they can burst into flames with little warning. This issue was in the news in late 2015 after thousands of kids received hoverboards for Christmas. Although the self-balancing electric scooters were one of the most popular gifts of the holiday season, several hoverboards exploded and burned down houses in New York and Louisiana. Another hoverboard started a fire in a mall in Auburn, Washington, forcing an evacuation. The danger is considered serious enough that major airlines have banned hoverboards from all flights.

ion

An atom or molecule with an electric charge caused by the loss or gain of one or more electrons.

The problems were caused by the highly volatile lithium used in the hoverboard batteries. If a li-ion battery is jolted or exposed to high heat, it can become damaged. This leads to a short circuit, which causes the battery to explode; lithium burns fast and hot, and the fires are difficult to contain. Because the hoverboards were so popular, dozens of manufacturers rushed inexpensive models into stores with cheap batteries that were prone to problems.

Another problem with li-ion batteries is familiar to anyone who owns a cell phone, tablet computer, or laptop. The batteries run down rather quickly and take a long time to recharge. Moreover, the batteries become less powerful after one hundred charges and can fail completely after three hundred to five hundred charges.

Hoverboards like the one pictured here have been known to cause serious fires when the volatile li-ion batteries that power them have unexpectedly burst into flames. These led to major airlines banning the boards from their flights as a safety precaution.

Long-Lasting, Superfast Charging

Researchers are working to create a new generation of li-ion batteries that are safer, longer lasting, and more powerful. They are doing so by examining each part of the battery, working to improve cathodes, anodes, electrolyte, and other battery elements. For example, scientists at Nanyang Technology University (NTU) in Singapore have reinvented the anode to create a long-lasting battery that charges very quickly.

The anodes in li-ion batteries are made from graphite, the same form of carbon used in most pencils. Most graphite is mined in China, where graphite pollution has become a serious problem. Small particles of graphite pollute the air, water, and soil and cause health problems for miners. And graphite mining by-products include toxic acids and heavy metals like lead. The batteries in a typical electric car contain 110 pounds (50 kg) of graphite, and a laptop battery contains about 3.5 ounces (100 gm).

Researchers at NTU replaced the graphite anode with a gel made from titanium dioxide, a safe and abundant material found in soil and commonly used in sunscreen lotions. The scientists converted the titanium dioxide particles into tiny structures called nanotubes. These tubular molecules, a thousand times thinner than a human hair, are used in dozens of applications, including electronics, medicine, energy, and even fashion. Nanotubes are excellent at conducting electricity, can withstand high temperatures, and are incredibly strong for their tiny size and weight.

electrode

One of the two points through which electricity flows into or out of a battery.

When used in batteries, titanium dioxide nanotubes speed up chemical reactions in the electrolyte, which allows for superfast charging. A titanium dioxide battery large enough to power an electric car can be partially charged in five minutes and fully charged in twelve minutes. This compares very favorably to the li-ion batteries in most electric cars, which can take four hours to recharge. Additionally, batteries with titanium dioxide nanotubes have a much longer life; they can endure ten thousand charging cycles. That means a titanium dioxide battery could be recharged every day for twenty-seven years.

Professor Chen Xiaodong, who is leading the research at NTU, expects titanium dioxide will replace graphite anodes in li-ion batteries by 2020. Chen explains the advantages of the new battery:

> With our nanotechnology, electric cars would be able to increase their range dramatically with just five minutes of charging, which is on par with the time needed to pump

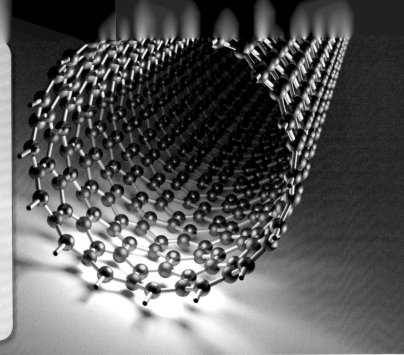

This computer-generated rendering depicts a carbon nanotube. Scientists are seeking to use similar structures made from titanium dioxide in batteries to replace li-ion batteries. Titanium dioxide nanotubes would enable these new batteries to charge faster and last much longer than the li-ion type.

[gasoline] for current cars. Equally important, we can now drastically cut down the waste generated by disposed batteries, since our batteries last . . . longer than the current generation of lithium-ion batteries.[8]

Hemp Super Batteries

Scientists are also turning to nanotechnology to improve batteries known as supercapacitors, or supercaps. Supercaps can be charged instantly and suffer very little degradation over time. Researchers hope to use them one day in electric cars, buses, trains, and other heavy-use applications. The problem is that supercaps are not energy dense—they hold 95 percent less energy than a li-ion battery. However, the energy density of supercaps can be improved if the electrodes are made with an extremely thin substance called graphene, which is made from graphite.

Graphene is a solid, light material made of a layer of carbon called a nanosheet, which is only one molecule in thickness. But there are problems with graphene: production of graphene nanosheets is very polluting. The process requires a very strong acid, such as sulfuric acid, to strip the graphene from graphite. However, researchers have discovered that graphene can be replaced with nonpolluting hemp fibers to make organic supercap nanosheets.

Hemp is a variety of the cannabis plant, which is biologically related to marijuana. Hemp has very low levels of THC, the psycho-active ingredient in marijuana. Whereas marijuana has 5 to 25 percent THC content, hemp only has about .3 percent. Although people cannot use hemp to get high, federal law in the United States prohibits farmers from growing hemp. In China, Canada, and the United Kingdom, hemp can be grown industrially for clothing and building materials. In the United States, hemp products, including rope, paper, cloth, oil, and food seeds, are legal to possess.

nanosheet

An extremely thin molecular structure that contains only a single layer of atoms.

David Mitlin, a professor at Clarkson University in New York, discovered that hemp nanosheets perform as well as graphene but are a thousand times cheaper to produce. Hemp nanosheet production does not require polluting acid, and hemp can be grown without herbicides and chemical fertilizers. Additionally, the nanosheets are made from the inner fibers of hemp, called bast, which is considered a waste product and is usually dumped in landfills. Mitlin's team took bast and recycled it into supercapacitors. According to Mitlin, "Fifty miles down the road from my house in Alberta [Canada] there was an agricultural hemp processing facility. And all that bast fiber—they don't know what to do with it. It's a waste product looking for a value-added application. People are almost paying you to take it away."[9] Mitlin plans to start a company to produce supercap nanosheets with the hemp waste.

Sugar-Filled Bio-Batteries

Nonpolluting organic substances are also being used to create electrolyte in biological batteries, or bio-batteries. These batteries produce electricity by mimicking the ways plants and animals

Cigarette-Butt Batteries

Cigarette butts are the most common form of litter—an estimated 1.7 billion pounds (771 million kg) of butts wind up as toxic litter every year. But in 2014 researchers at Seoul National University in South Korea discovered a way to convert used cigarette filters into supercapacitors that charge quicker and last longer than li-ion batteries. Cigarette filters are the part of the cigarette that people hold between their lips. They are made from a nonbiodegradable material called cellulose acetate. Researchers found they could convert cellulose acetate into carbon by heating it at 1,652°F (900°C) for two hours.

Carbon conducts electricity well, which makes it the most popular material for making supercapacitors. According to Korean scientists, the butt-based material was able to charge faster and hold a charge longer than other substances used in supercapacitors, including graphene. And whereas graphene is expensive to produce, used cigarette butts are free.

create energy. The key to producing bio-batteries is finding a way to utilize glucose. This common sugar fuels all living things, including plants, people, and animals. All parts of the human body, including the muscles, brain, heart, and other organs, need energy to function. The energy comes from food that is broken down into glucose by molecules in the stomach called enzymes. During the digestion process, the enzymes create energy to power the body. A bio-battery imitates the digestion process, using enzymes to produce electricity.

Research into bio-batteries is being conducted by biology professor Y.H. Percival Zhang at Virginia Tech. The bio-battery works with maltodextrin, a glucose substance derived from corn or wheat; it is commonly used in soda, candy, and processed foods. The battery passes maltodextrin through a pathway lined with enzymes that strip the sugar of its energy while generating electricity.

The sugar battery has about ten times the energy density of a li-ion battery, which means it can go much longer between charges. And whereas billions of li-ion batteries end up in landfills every year, sugar batteries can remain in use for years. When the sugar batteries lose capacity, they can be refilled with powdered maltodextrin the same way that printer cartridges are refilled with ink. As Zhang points out, "Sugar is a perfect energy storage compound in nature. So it's only logical that we try to harness this natural power in an environmentally friendly way to produce a battery."[10] Zhang believes sugar batteries could replace li-ions in cell phones and laptops by 2020.

electrolyte

A liquid in a battery through which electricity passes.

Sugar batteries might even have applications for use in the human body. Researchers at the Massachusetts Institute of Technology (MIT) have developed a tiny glucose-powered battery for medical use. There are hopes that the battery can be implanted in the brains of people with spinal cord injuries resulting in paralyzed limbs. According to Benjamin I. Rapoport, an MIT engineer who worked on the battery, "It will be a few more years into the future before you see people with spinal-cord injuries receive such implantable systems in the context of standard medical care, but those are the sorts of devices you could envision powering from a glucose-based [battery]."[11]

Foldable Batteries

While some researchers are working to improve electrolyte and electrodes, others are rethinking the entire design and structure of the battery to make it more versatile. One futuristic battery is based on the ancient Japanese art of origami, or paper folding. In 2013 researchers at Arizona State University created a li-ion battery that can be folded, twisted, and scrunched into various shapes. The origami batteries are meant to work with flexible electronics such as extremely thin smartphones that can be bent, rolled, or folded.

The origami battery is based on the Miura fold. This intricate fold was invented in 1995 by Japanese astrophysicist Koryo Miura. It was intended to be used on space-saving foldable solar

Although electrodes made of graphene (pictured) can improve the energy density of batteries known as supercapacitors, producing the substance is very polluting. For that reason, scientists are looking into ways to make organic electrodes from fibers derived from the hemp plant.

panels on spacecraft. Arizona researchers applied the Miura fold to a battery that performs as well as a standard rigid, block-shaped li-ion battery.

Researchers say the origami battery will someday be used on flexible and wearable computers. For example, the battery could be placed on the strap of a smartwatch, which would allow the watch mechanism to be much thinner. The batteries could also be used in athletic wear known as smart clothing, which tracks a person's workout with sensors that measure distances, calories burned, and heart rate. Since origami batteries can be stretched to more than 150 percent of their original size, the batteries could be sewn into the stretchy fabrics of smart clothing, including shirts, shorts, and running shoes.

Textile Batteries

Scientists at Fudan University in Shanghai, China, have taken the idea of the origami battery one step further. In 2014 they created a high-performance battery yarn that can be weaved into textiles. The li-ion battery is made of carbon nanotube fibers that are little more than .03 inches (.08 cm) in diameter.

The lightweight, flexible yarn can create power-providing textiles. Fudan battery researcher Wei Wang explains the uses for his creation: "We want to create clothes and blankets to charge our daily electronics [such as] mobile phones. We also see them as an emergency energy source when you hike or camp. . . . Or the textile batteries could directly be woven into your sleeping bag or tent."[12]

Photoswitching

Although many cutting edge batteries are designed to produce electricity, a new source of power being developed at MIT and Harvard University is known as a thermal battery. The thermal battery stores heat from the sun in a chemical compound called azobenzene, which has an unusual trait: molecules of azobenzene switch shape when exposed to the sun.

Scientists refer to the azobenzene molecules as photoswitches. A statement released by MIT researchers explains how they work: "Photoswitches can assume either of two different shapes, as if they had a hinge in the middle. Exposing them to sunlight causes them to absorb energy and jump from one [shape] to the other."[13] When they switch shape, the molecules generate heat that can be harnessed to provide power.

Researchers are hoping to create a liquid filled with photoswitching molecules. The liquid would be used in a system consisting of two tanks connected by a clear tube. The photoswitching liquid would be pumped through the tube, where it would be charged during exposure to sunlight. The charged liquid would then be stored in the second tank for use when the sun is not shining. As MIT professor of materials science Jeffery Grossman explains, photoswitching "could change the [energy] game, since it makes the sun's energy, in the form of heat, storable and distributable."[14]

The technology would be particularly useful in developing countries where people burn wood to cook and heat their homes.

Potato Power

One of the most basic science fair experiments involves making a battery from a potato. With copper wire and zinc-coated nails acting as electrodes, a raw potato can provide power to a small clock or light. The potato itself is not an energy source; it works as the electrolyte that separates the zinc and copper electrodes. In 2013 researchers at Hebrew University in Jerusalem took the science fair potato battery project to the next level. Scientists discovered that a boiled potato provides ten times the power of a raw one, and cutting up the boiled potato makes it even more powerful. The researchers placed a boiled potato slice between copper cathodes and zinc anodes to create a device that can power an LED light for up to forty days. Potatoes are 90 percent cheaper than AA batteries, and the Jerusalem scientists believe potatoes could supply power for cell phones, radios, and lights in underdeveloped nations where there is little access to the power grid.

Potatoes are composed of a starch that can be stored for months without attracting insects. Potatoes are also the world's fourth most-abundant crop. The main drawback is that food-based energy systems are not useful in places where food is scarce. Hungry people would rather eat a potato than use it to light their homes.

This results in deforestation when trees are cut down and air pollution when the wood is burned. Both activities contribute to climate change. However, a photoswitching stove could be placed in the sun all day and used at night when it was time to cook dinner.

Photoswitches could be used for heating buildings and providing heat to industrial manufacturing processes. Unlike fuels that are burned, the photoswitching system uses material that can be continually reused. It produces no emissions, and nothing gets consumed.

Powering Up

Developing new sources of battery power might take on a greater urgency if electric vehicles someday replace most gasoline-powered cars. Although such a change would reduce the threat of climate change, the switch to electric vehicles would greatly increase the demand for lithium. The battery pack in a large electric car like a Tesla Model S uses 22 pounds (10 kg) of lithium. About 80 million new cars are produced every year throughout the world. If they all used li-ion batteries, researchers believe there would be a severe lithium shortage.

Because lithium is a finite resource, like oil, the move is on to diversify battery production with both common and exotic materials. When people of the future are powering up their phones, stoves, and cars, they will likely be using the next generation of batteries to provide the juice.

CHAPTER THREE

Microbe Power

One of the many challenges facing society is how to dispose of the mountains of organic waste produced by animals and people every day. According to the US Environmental Protection Agency (EPA), organic material such as rotting food, animal manure, and sewer sludge makes up the largest and heaviest portion of the waste stream in the United States. Most waste is simply dumped in landfills or bulldozed into pits where the material releases methane, a greenhouse gas that contributes to climate change.

Yet organic waste does not have to be a pollution problem; methane is a rich source of clean energy called biogas. This was noted by President Barack Obama in the 2013 report *Climate Action Plan—Strategy to Reduce Methane Emissions.* Obama's plan calls on the US government to develop a "strategy to reduce methane emissions and promote cutting-edge technologies that help farmers, energy companies, and communities convert methane into a renewable energy source and grow America's biogas energy industry."[15]

Gas Recovery

The process of turning waste into energy is based on the concept of anaerobic digestion. *Anaerobic* means "living without air." During anaerobic digestion, microbes (or microorganisms) break down organic material in the absence of oxygen. The human body contains trillions of microbes. Some digest the food people eat, converting it into energy and excrement in the absence of air.

Microbes also consume garbage, food scraps, animal manure, and other organic material. During the process, microbes produce biogas consisting of methane (CH_4), carbon dioxide (CO_2), and water. When the process occurs naturally—in a garbage can, landfill, or barn—the gases escape into the atmosphere.

Scientists have devised processes whereby anaerobic digestion occurs in a controlled environment called a biogas recovery system (BRS). The methane produced during the anaerobic digestion process is similar to natural gas in its chemical composition. Like natural gas, biogas can be used as transportation fuel or burned to generate heat or electricity.

There are two main benefits to biogas recovery systems. They make use of products like rotting food and manure that otherwise are considered worthless. And BRSs are good for the environment; biogas contains between 50 and 70 percent methane, the second most-prevalent greenhouse gas after carbon

biogas

Methane fuel produced through the fermentation of organic matter.

dioxide. According to the EPA, methane's lifetime in the atmosphere is much shorter than CO_2, but it is more efficient at trapping heat in the atmosphere. This makes methane twenty-five times more harmful than CO_2. Capturing and using methane as an energy source is important for slowing climate change. Robert Howarth, a professor of ecology and environmental biology, states, "If we cut methane emissions now, we can slow the rate of [global] warming almost immediately."[16]

Energy from Livestock Waste

A typical biogas recovery system contains a tank that looks like a small grain silo. Farmers dump animal manure into the tank, where naturally occurring bacteria break down the waste. As the Dairy Doing More website explains, "On the farm, raw manure is treated inside a heated, oxygen-free container that essentially continues the digestion that began in the cow's stomach."[17]

The anaerobic digestion process produces liquids, solids, and methane gas. The process removes much of the odor from the liquid, which is used as an environmentally friendly crop fertilizer. The biogas can be diverted to tanks for later use in heating, cooking, or powering natural gas vehicles. The gas can also be piped as fuel to a small electrical generator or to an electrical power plant. The odor-reduced solids left behind are used for compost, potting soil, and dairy bedding.

Tons of garbage are dumped every day in landfills like the one pictured here. Both to combat pollution and generate energy, scientists are researching ways to use microbes to break down organic waste into biogas, which can be used as fuel.

Dairy cows create a huge amount of waste. A single cow produces 120 pounds (54 kg) of manure and urine a day. One dairy farm with twenty-five hundred cows produces as much waste as a city with around 411,000 residents. Whereas cities are required by law to treat sewage with chemicals and filtration before releasing it into the environment, most farms are not. Animal waste is most often dumped in giant outdoor pits known as lagoons. All animal waste lagoons leak to some degree, and some overflow during severe storms. Occasionally the lagoons break and spill their contents into waterways. Likewise, the lagoons release methane and CO_2 into the air as well as toxic, and smelly, ammonia and hydrogen sulfide gases. This is prompting some farmers to install biogas recovery systems to convert animal waste to energy.

Obama's *Climate Action Plan* calls for the construction of eleven thousand biogas recovery systems for use on farms. If fully implemented, the biogas systems would produce enough energy to power more than 3 million American homes and would reduce methane emissions equivalent to removing approximately 5 million passenger vehicles from the road.

Dog Waste to Energy

Although most people would rather not think about it, dog waste is a huge problem: America's 83 million pet dogs produce 10.6 million tons (9.6 million metric tons) of poop every year. That is enough to fill a line of semitrucks stretching from Boston to Seattle. And studies have traced 20 to 30 percent of the harmful bacteria in urban water to dog waste. Only around 50 percent of dog owners even bother to pick up their dog's waste. Those who do clean up after their dogs usually place the waste in nonbiodegradable plastic grocery bags that end up in landfills. But the same system that recovers biogas from livestock manure can turn dog poop into power.

Several cities are acting to solve their dog waste problems. In San Francisco, dog waste makes up 4 percent of the city's waste stream. This has prompted the city to build an anaerobic digester to process organic waste, including droppings from the city's 120,000 dogs. In Toronto, curbside bins are used to collect dog poop. The waste is fed into an anaerobic digester to produce energy. In Gilbert, Arizona, local students raised funds to build an underground anaerobic digester in the city's dog park, which 200 dogs visit daily. The digester, called eTURD, provides gas to a streetlight in the park that is lit by a flame of burning methane generated by the local dogs.

However, a BRS does not make financial sense for the majority of American farmers. In addition to the large upfront costs, most utilities are not willing to pay enough for electricity generated by relatively small systems. A BRS also requires a great deal of maintenance, and many farms do not have the extra laborers to service the complex machinery. Because of the costs and other difficulties, only around 250 biogas recovery systems operated on farms in the United States in 2015. Nonetheless, the EPA estimates that even this small number is helping the environment. The BRSs eliminate more than 3 million tons (2.7 million metric tons) of greenhouse gas emissions, the equivalent of taking 630,000 cars off the road.

Food Power

Biogas recovery systems do not have to be confined to farms. Anaerobic digesters work with any organic material and can be extremely beneficial in urban areas. People in big cities produce mountains of garbage—called municipal solid waste (MSW)—on a daily basis. In the United States, 250 million tons (226.7 million metric tons) of garbage is disposed of every year.

Americans throw out about 40 percent of the food they purchase annually. This adds up to around 14 percent, or 37.5 million tons (34 million metric tons), of all MSW. Another 13 percent of garbage produced is yard waste, which includes grass, leaves, and tree and brush trimmings. When yard waste and food are dumped in landfills, the materials rot, releasing methane. For this reason, about one hundred American cities have launched recycling programs to keep food and yard waste out of landfills. In doing so, they are turning garbage into gold.

The city of San Jose, California, has taken food and yard waste recycling a step further. San Jose, located 48 miles (77 km) south of San Francisco, opened the Zero Waste Energy Development (ZWED) facility in 2013. ZWED is the first large-scale commercial anaerobic digestion facility in the United States and the largest such operation in the world. During its first year of operation in 2014, ZWED recycled more than 36,000 tons (32,658 metric tons) of organic waste from San Jose and nearby cities. The food and yard waste was processed in sixteen anaerobic digesters, which use bacteria to break down the waste in a process that takes three weeks. During its first year ZWED captured 125 million cubic feet (3.5 million cu m) of methane. Some of the gas fueled the company's garbage trucks, which had been converted to run on methane gas. The rest of the methane fueled an onsite generator that provided ZWED with all its power. The facility also produced approximately 6,000 tons (5,443 metric tons) of compost that was sold to farmers and gardeners.

In 2015 ZWED made plans to expand to more than seven times its original size. When fully operational, the plant will be one of the largest biogas production systems in the world, processing

A machine pumps sludge from a lagoon holding animal waste. Biogas recovery systems are capable of converting animal waste to energy, but the systems are too expensive and require too much maintenance to be cost effective for most American farmers.

up to 270,000 tons (245,000 metric tons) of food and yard waste a year. ZWED plans to sell its excess power to the huge California utility Pacific Gas & Electric (PG&E). Julia Levin, director of the Bioenergy Association of California, explains the advantages of large-scale biogas systems: "In the long run, there's a lot of potential for biogas to be used as transportation fuel. San Jose is on the cutting edge, but cities across California are trying to figure out how to better handle their waste. Biogas closes the sustainability loop on so many levels."[18]

Sludge Power

San Jose is not the only city trying to find innovative ways to reuse waste. Los Angeles, which is California's biggest city, is working with the county sewage treatment plant to recycle its food waste. In early 2014 Los Angeles began a program to collect food scraps from restaurants, hotels, grocery stores, and food-processing plants. The food is trucked to a facility in Carson, located 13 miles

(21 km) south of Los Angeles. The food waste is ground into a semisolid slurry that is transported to the Los Angeles County wastewater treatment facility (WWTF).

Like the other twelve hundred wastewater treatment facilities in the United States, the one in Los Angeles County uses physical, chemical, and biological processes to clean up household sewage. The plants remove pollutants and solids and break down organic matter. When the process is complete, there are two products: wastewater solids, called sludge, and clean water, which is usually returned to local waterways.

sludge

A semisolid material that is a by-product of sewage created in wastewater treatment plants.

In past decades sewer sludge was trucked to local landfills. Yet in recent years around 860 wastewater plants in the United States have been using the sludge to produce biogas. The Los Angeles County WWTF mixes nine parts sludge with one part food-waste slurry brought in from Carson. This is fed into an anaerobic digester. Since food waste is richer in organic matter, it produces several times more methane than manure or sewage.

Food and Sewage

Whereas the Los Angeles facility uses the biogas as fuel for plant operations, another California WWTF is making a profit on its food and sludge power. The East Bay Municipal Utility District, which serves Oakland, Berkeley, and surrounding communities, creates so much energy through anaerobic codigestion that it sells power to PG&E. In 2013 the plant made about $1 million selling surplus energy.

The concept of converting food scraps to power is catching on in other states. Connecticut, Massachusetts, and Vermont have banned commercial food producers from dumping waste in landfills. The states have set up codigestion programs to produce energy at WWTFs. In central Florida, a facility codigests sewage and food waste from nearby businesses, including Disney World.

Beer, Brewing, and Biogas

Waste-to-energy systems are very popular in Europe. There are around fourteen thousand municipally operated biogas digesters, with nine thousand of them in Germany alone. Germany is also famous for its beer, but the by-products of the brewing process are often viewed as a nuisance by brewers. Most German beer is made with barley, although some styles also use wheat. When the process is complete, brewers are left with tons of sodden grain. For centuries the grain was either used as livestock feed or spread on fields as fertilizer. However, in 2000 Germany enacted strict regulations on what types of waste would be allowed on land; because of the air and water pollution problems associated with rotting grain, brewers were prohibited from using beer waste for agricultural purposes. Breweries were forced to pay to dispose of their mountains of spent grain.

Where brewers saw a costly problem, researcher Wolfgang Bengel saw an opportunity. Bengel is the technical director of BMP Biomasse Projekt, a German biomass company. He started his career working in China and Thailand, where he used waste from rice and sugarcane production to produce energy with biogas digesters. Bengel realized he could put the concept to work for brewers.

The process begins with the used grain being mixed with wastewater from the brewing process. The soup is placed in a fermenter with bacteria that breaks down the grain and produces methane and a dried sludge. The resulting biogas and the sludge is burned to boil water. The steam turns an electrical turbine to generate about half the power needed by the brewery. The process can save brewers a great deal of money, as Bengel explains: "Beer making is energy intensive—you boil stuff, use hot water and steam and then use electric energy for cooling—so if you recover more than 50 percent of your own energy costs from the spent grain, that's a big saving."[19]

Electric Microbes

Biogas systems for breweries have a large footprint—they take up valuable floor space and might even require a separate building.

Bottles of beer on an assembly line pass through a brewery. German researcher Wolfgang Bengel developed a way to produce methane and sludge from beer-making waste products, then burn them to produce steam that turns an electrical turbine and generates electricity. This process can produce about half the energy needed to power a brewery.

But a California company called Cambrian Innovation believes it has solved the space problem for smaller breweries, or micro-breweries. Cambrian's EcoVolt machine fits inside standard 40-foot (12 m) shipping containers, steel boxes like those seen on big eighteen-wheeler trucks.

The EcoVolt extracts energy from industrial wastewater cre-ated by breweries and food and beverage producers. Like the thickened liquid in soup, the wastewater is filled with organic materials. However, wastewater has a very low oxygen content, which can harm fish and other aquatic animals. As such, indus-trial wastewater cannot be drained into municipal sewers. Food and beverage producers are required by law to pump air into, or aerate, the water. The pumps use a lot of electricity, and this is where the EcoVolt comes into play.

The EcoVolt reactor does not work the same way as a typical BRS; it works like a giant battery in a complex process that takes place on a microbial level. The EcoVolt contains a particular type of microbe that produces electrons during anaerobic digestion. These microbes, which were discovered in soil in South Korea in 2010, are called exoelectrogens, or anode-respiring bacteria.

Methane and Clean Water

In technical terms, the EcoVolt is a microbial fuel cell, or a bioelectric system. In the EcoVolt, the microbes create electrons as they consume the organic material in the wastewater. The electrons are deposited on a special anode covered with bacterial film. The electrons flow between the anode and a cathode, producing hydrogen and CO_2. The EcoVolt converts these chemicals into methane, which can then be burned to produce heat or electricity.

exoelectrogens

Microorganisms that have the ability to generate electricity by creating electrons during anaerobic digestion.

The EcoVolt leaves behind clean water as a by-product while reducing the need to generate electricity with fossil fuels. About 3 percent of all electricity consumed in the United States is used to treat wastewater. And the production of one bottle of beer creates ten bottles of wastewater. The benefits of extracting clean water and energy from waste can be seen at the Bear Republic Brewery in Cloverdale, California. In 2014 Bear Republic installed two EcoVolt systems. The microbial fuel cells reduced the brewery's energy costs associated with wastewater treatment by 80 to 90 percent. Additionally, the EcoVolt systems allow the brewery to reuse 10 percent of its wastewater, and the biogas creates 50 percent of the brewery's electricity. The bioelectric systems will pay for themselves in five years. A similar system is in place at the Clos du Bois winery in Sonoma County, California. Matthew Silver, CEO of Cambrian Innovation, explains the value of his microbial fuel cells: "Up until now, compliance (with water treatment regulations) was viewed as a cost of doing business. . . . Now wastewater can be a source of revenue."[20]

The Poo Bus

In March 2015 Bristol, England, became the first city to power public transportation with human waste. Bristol's forty-seat Bio-Bus fuels up every day at the city's sewage treatment plant, where human waste and food scraps are converted into methane gas by an anaerobic digester. The engine of the Bio-Bus runs quieter than a diesel-fueled bus, and the exhaust from the clean burning natural gas does not smell.

The Bio-Bus is entirely fueled by the food waste and sewage of Bristol's thirty-two thousand households. A single tank of the biogas, which powers the vehicle for 190 miles (306 km), is produced by the annual waste of five people. And those who live along the bus's service route produce enough waste to run a Bio-Bus for 2.5 million miles (4.1 million km) a year. Although the bus only travels a fraction of that distance, it is seen as a useful tool to remind people to recycle their food waste. As bus company worker Colin Field states, "When they can actually see that the waste they put in their little [garbage] bin . . . is powering this vehicle, it makes people look at it in a slightly different light."

Another thing riders see in a different light is the Bio-Bus itself. Locals refer to the vehicle as "the Poo Bus." And if the Poo Bus proves to be successful, the city is planning to put an entire fleet of Bio-Buses into service.

Quoted in Eleanor Goldberg, "The Public Bus Runs Entirely on Human Poop Converted into Fuel," Huffington Post, March 18, 2015. www.huffingtonpost.com.

Harvesting Electrons

Microbial fuel cells might someday be fueled by plants. The roots of living plants cast off numerous waste products, such as glucose and acetate. When these by-products are anaerobically consumed by microbes, the process leaves electrons in the surrounding soil and water.

Dutch researchers at Wageningen University in the Netherlands have discovered a way to use plant electrons to produce power. They planted a plot of grass on the roof of a university building and used specially designed equipment to generate a low amount of power from the plant roots. Although the technology is in its infancy, researchers hope that grassy generators on rooftops will someday power the buildings they sit atop.

Plants, like people, generate waste products that are often overlooked in the quest to create renewable energy. But there is energy to be found in almost every environment, from the forest to the barn and brewery. While the by-products of urban, agricultural, and industrial society have long been seen as trash, there is heat and power to be harvested from the waste. Although dealing with manure, trash, and sewage is a dirty business, the microbes that make all life on Earth possible are being put to work to turn crud into cash.

CHAPTER FOUR

Green Buildings

According to the industry group US Green Building Council, the "green" building trade is one of the fastest-growing industries worldwide. Between 2009 and 2015 the number of architects, engineers, and contractors worldwide who said they were working with green designs more than doubled from 13 percent to 28 percent. These pioneers of sustainable architecture are turning tradition on its head. They are shifting away from standard building materials while adopting new construction techniques to create super energy-efficient residential and commercial structures. Some of the materials are not exactly new—in the way that materials created through nanotechnology, for instance, are new. Rather, the pioneering designers and builders are turning to materials not traditionally used in building construction, such as recycled steel, aluminum, and even used car tires. Builders are also experimenting with new construction techniques, building homes into hillsides and even making plans to turn trees into living buildings.

The goal of sustainable architecture is to dramatically reduce the amount of energy used in homes and businesses. In the United States, cars, trucks, trains, and airplanes account for about 30 percent of the nation's overall energy consumption. Even more energy—41 percent—is used to heat, cool, and light homes and commercial buildings. About 7 percent of this power comes from renewable sources like solar and wind. But a large chunk of the energy consumed in homes, offices, apartments, and stores is provided by fossil fuels. Nearly 40 percent of America's electricity comes from coal, and 38 percent is generated by natural gas. About half of all US homes use natural gas for heating and cooking; the rest use fuel oil, propane, or electricity.

Green building designers try to make the structures carbon neutral—meaning their energy consumption is so low the buildings produce zero carbon dioxide and therefore do not contribute to global warming. Some cutting edge green buildings are even better than carbon neutral. They produce more electricity than the structure uses, energy that can be fed into the power grid for use elsewhere.

Sustainable Building Materials

Green designers often work to incorporate recycled materials into structures. As the National Recycling Coalition states, sustainable materials benefit the environment because "manufacturing recycled products requires, on average, 17 times less energy than manufacturing the same products from virgin materials."[21] This is behind the move to use recycled steel to replace the wood typically used to frame houses. Steel-framed structures are stronger; more resistant to fires, mold, and insects; and require less maintenance. According to the National Recycling Coalition, there is a 75 percent energy savings with recycled steel compared with new steel; for each ton of steel that is recycled, 1,000 pounds (453 kg) of coal is not burned. Whereas six scrapped cars can provide enough steel to build a home, a typical wood home requires cutting down forty to sixty trees. If left in the ground, each tree would absorb as much as 48 pounds (22 kg) of carbon dioxide per year through the act of photosynthesis, in which plants consume CO_2 while producing oxygen.

carbon neutral

When energy consumption is so low that a building produces zero carbon dioxide and therefore does not contribute to global warming.

Other recycled materials not commonly used for construction can be surprisingly sturdy and beautiful. The architectural firm Archi Union used thousands of aluminum soft drink cans to build the three-story, multiuse Can Cube building in Shanghai in 2010. The Can Cube's facade consists of a system of aluminum frames enclosing the empty drink cans. Ordinarily, aluminum cans are melted down during the recycling process. But according to the architects, "The façade [of the Can Cube] saves the energy wasted during recycling processes by reusing the cans in their current form, without the need for recycling or further processes."[22] The

Architect Michael E. Reynolds discovered that dirt-filled scrap tires make inexpensive and durable home foundations and walls. Here, workers use these materials to construct one of Reynolds' dwellings, which he calls Earthships.

first story of the Can Cube contains office space, and the second and third floors are recreational and private living quarters. Can Cube residents rely on solar energy for electricity and a rainwater filtration system for freshwater.

"Radically Sustainable" Earthships

Architect Michael E. Reynolds understands the value of recycled materials. His unique homes, called Earthships, are made with scrap tires—a type of garbage that creates problems almost everywhere. Old car and truck tires have created an environmental disaster. The United States alone produces about 250 million scrap tires a year, and millions are illegally dumped. Scrap tires fill with rainwater and provide breeding grounds for mosquitos. Tire piles sometimes catch on fire and, because of the burning rubber and steel, these fires can be very difficult to put out. Even when tires are recycled, fossil fuels are needed to process them into other products. But in the early 2000s Reynolds discovered that layers of old tires filled with dirt make inexpensive, well-insulated, and nearly indestructible walls for his Earthship houses. Reynolds describes the houses as "radically sustainable."[23]

In 2015 about seventy Earthships dotted the sagebrush-covered hills around Taos, New Mexico. The homes range in size from 2,200 to 5,400 square feet (204 to 502 sq m). Earthships are earth-sheltered homes—three sides of the structure are underground, usually sunk into a hill. This provides maximum insulation, as Reynolds explains:

> The outer few feet of the earth heats up and cools off in response to surface weather. However, deeper in the earth, about four feet and beyond, the temperature is more constant (around 58 degrees). Here, the earth can be used to both cool and stabilize temperature if the home is appropriately designed. . . . Because of the way Earthships interact with the sun and the earth, little to no fossil fuels are required to maintain a comfortable, stable temperature in any climate.[24]

All Earthships face south to take advantage of the sun's warming rays. The front part of the home consists of a long, open corridor with huge windows. All rooms are located in a line along the corridor. This provides maximum exposure to the sun and eliminates the need for heating and interior lighting during the day.

Solar panels and small wind turbines create the electricity needed for Earthships. Water conservation is also important in this arid region of New Mexico. The roofs of Earthships catch rain and snowmelt, which is stored in cisterns. The water is filtered and used for drinking, washing, and bathing. All Earthships have large food gardens. One Taos Earthship, called the Phoenix, produces a grocery list of food that includes broccoli, peppers, corn, tomatoes, lemons, oranges, coconuts, bananas, grapes, and enough herbs to fill a spice cabinet. Earthship gardens are watered with gray water—filtered water from the shower, laundry, and kitchen.

cistern

A tank or underground reservoir used for storing water.

The Greenest Skyscraper

Skyscrapers and high-rise buildings can be energy hogs. Tall buildings jut hundreds of feet into the air, and their plateglass windows are all that stand between high winds, intense sunlight, and winter cold. People living and working in a skyscraper often need to keep the lights on during the day since many rooms inside the building have no natural light. Yet this does not have to be the case. Even skyscrapers can be designed to work with nature.

The thirty-three-story Tower at PNC Plaza in Pittsburgh, Pennsylvania, is classified as the greenest skyscraper ever built. The $400 million corporate headquarters for PNC Bank was completed in 2015 with numerous sustainable elements. The Tower is designed with windows and floor plans that take advantage of natural light, and the building harvests rainwater so that it uses 77 percent less water than a typical office building of similar size.

The Tower is ventilated with a feature called a solar chimney, which is made from two panes of exterior glass separated by an enclosed cavity. When the sun hits the solar chimney, it pulls cooler air into the cavity. The air in the chimney flows into and out of the building through operable doors and windows. This movement ventilates the building without the use of huge fans, which sit atop most skyscrapers, and provides natural ventilation to the Tower around six months out of the year.

Earthships are known as zero-energy buildings (ZEBs); no outside sources of power are required to provide the buildings with their energy needs. Additionally, the homes do not require any other public utility hookups, as Reynolds explains:

There's nothing coming into this house, no power lines, no gas lines, no sewage lines coming out, no water lines coming in, no energy being used. We're sitting on 6,000 gallons of [stored] water, growing food . . . the home is 70 degrees [21°C] year-round. What these kind of houses are doing is taking every aspect of your life and putting it into your own hands. A family of four could totally survive here without having to go to the store.[25]

Since 2007 Reynolds has been exporting the Earthship designs to communities in countries throughout the world. The houses work in most any climate; currently they are found in Africa, Asia, Australia, New Zealand, Europe, the United States, and Central and South America.

Energy-Plus Houses

Self-sufficient housing is one of a variety of ideas being pursued by green builders. Another is known as an energy-plus house. This is a house that produces more power than it needs. The surplus electricity is often enough to charge an electric car in the garage while also feeding power into the electric grid. One of the most advanced energy-plus experimental homes is located in Larvik, Norway. It was built by Norway's Research Centre on Zero Emission Buildings.

The Larvik energy-plus home is both beautiful and spacious—at 2,152 square feet (200 sq m) in size. The house is also a miniature power plant that produces twice as much energy as it consumes. Moreover, the energy-plus home is a portrait in simplicity. Whereas some high-tech energy-plus homes rely on computer sensors and fans to regulate the temperature, the Larvik home was built to take advantage of natural changes in wind and sunlight. For example, the roof is oddly tilted at a nineteen-degree angle. This design allows the rooftop solar panels to harvest the maximum amount of sunlight throughout the year. And the angled roof provides a natural updraft, which allows warm air to flow out of the building during Norway's long summer days. The Larvik home uses naturally generated heat in extremely efficient ways. The house is heated in the winter with energy from geothermal wells, or hot springs, which are located nearby. Excess indoor heat is channeled into the water heater, which provides hot tap water and also heats an outdoor swimming pool.

The Larvik Energy-Plus House

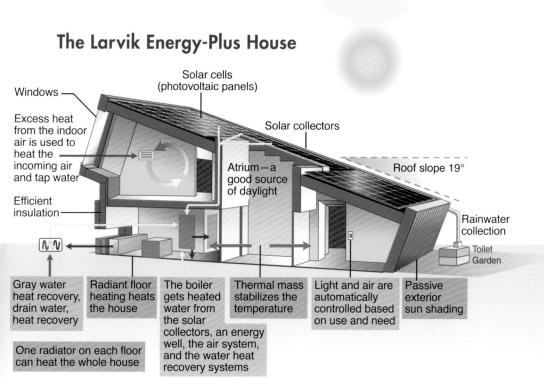

Windows

Excess heat from the indoor air is used to heat the incoming air and tap water

Efficient insulation

Solar cells (photovoltaic panels)

Solar collectors

Atrium—a good source of daylight

Roof slope 19°

Rainwater collection

Toilet
Garden

| Gray water heat recovery, drain water, heat recovery | Radiant floor heating heats the house | The boiler gets heated water from the solar collectors, an energy well, the air system, and the water heat recovery systems | Thermal mass stabilizes the temperature | Light and air are automatically controlled based on use and need | Passive exterior sun shading |

One radiator on each floor can heat the whole house

Source: E-Architect, "2EB Pilot House in Larvik," September 21, 2015. www.neat-living.com.

The energy-plus house was built using sustainable construction techniques. This means the project is 100 percent carbon neutral; no excess CO_2 was generated during its construction. The home's renewable energy generation helped offset the fossil fuels used to construct the building and to manufacture its solar panels, recycled steel frame, and appliances.

The lessons learned from building the Larvik pilot house are being put to use elsewhere in Norway. In 2015 a new development of eight hundred energy-plus homes was completed in Bergen. The homes are creating one problem, however: they produce so much power that the local utility company must devise an efficient way to feed the excess electricity into the grid.

Concrete from Hemp

Builders who wish to follow carbon-neutral construction principles are searching for alternatives to one of the most common

53

The Benefits of Green Walls

Green walls are the latest trend in energy-saving architecture. Since 2009, more than sixty large-scale outdoor green walls have been built around the world. Green walls can be seen on office buildings in San Francisco and at the airports in Mumbai, India, and Singapore.

Green walls are vertical gardens that include live plants and irrigation and drainage systems. In addition to adding beauty to a setting, the plants naturally filter harmful pollution from the air through photosynthesis. Green walls conserve energy by shading and adding insulation to a building. The walls also help save energy by reducing the effects of what is called the urban heat island—higher temperatures caused by a city's large expanse of asphalt, glass, steel, concrete, and brick. During the summer months, city temperatures can be two to eight degrees warmer than nearby rural areas. At night, the difference can be as high as twenty degrees. As temperatures rise, power plants have to keep up with the energy demand. But living walls work against the heat island effect. The plants cool themselves, lowering the temperature around the wall. This reduces the heat inside the building, thereby decreasing energy consumption. During the winter months, living walls provide extra insulation that prevents heat from escaping a building. The overall effect reduces energy costs and decreases carbon emissions.

building materials. Concrete is incredibly strong and durable and is used for foundations, driveways, patios, and sidewalks in millions of homes. But concrete is made with cement, a substance that sets and hardens the concrete. Cement is made by heating limestone to 2,642°F (1,450°C), and the process requires a great deal of fossil fuel. As a result, the cement industry produces about 5 percent of all global CO_2 emissions.

Researchers hoping to reduce or eliminate those emissions have turned to the versatile cannabis plant, or hemp. A product known as hempcrete (or hemcrete) is made from lime, water, and the soft inner core of the hemp stalk, called the hurd. The process does not require materials to be heated with fossil fuels.

Hempcrete does not require any change in standard concrete construction methods. To build a wall, workers create a plywood frame and pour the hemp-lime slurry into the form. This creates a thick concrete-like wall with a very high insulation value. In some tests, hempcrete saved homeowners 90 percent on their energy bills.

Hempcrete has other environmental benefits. Unlike many traditional home-building materials (such as plywood and insulation), hempcrete does not release toxic compounds into the air over time. Hempcrete also resists rotting, rodents and insects, and burning. And hempcrete is durable due to the fact that the calcium content of the lime calcifies, or hardens into a stone-like substance over time. Calcified hempcrete has been found in buildings that are thousands of years old in Asia and Africa. Studies in Europe have estimated that hempcrete walls have a life span of six hundred to eight hundred years.

calcify

The process in which calcium content in lime hardens into a stone-like substance over time.

Extreme strength is another attribute of hempcrete, which is around seven times stronger than concrete but weighs half as much. Hempcrete is also three times as elastic as concrete. This means that hempcrete foundations resist cracking and breaking, even in earthquake zones.

The Ashville Hemp House

Hemp hurds are being used to manufacture numerous building materials, including roofing tiles, wallboards, paneling, and insulation. Hempcrete is also used to make bricks. In Europe, where it is legal to grow hemp, hundreds of homes have been constructed with hemp building materials since the 1960s.

Although it is illegal to cultivate hemp in the United States, American suppliers can legally import hemp construction products. An eco-friendly construction company in Ashville, North Carolina, is taking advantage of that situation. In 2010 Push Design enlisted a team of forty volunteers—contractors, designers, and hemp promoters—to construct the first home in the United States primarily made from hemp.

Construction began with a foundation and 12-inch-thick (30 cm) outer walls made entirely from hempcrete. In keeping with carbon-neutral building techniques, the interior walls of the hemp house were lined with panels made entirely from recycled paper. This incredibly light building material was also used to make the interior doors. The window frames were recycled from demolished houses but were upgraded with heavier glass to provide better insulation.

The finished Hemp House is large, about 3,400 square feet (316 sq m). However, with its insulated windows and thick hempcrete walls, the heating and cooling bill is very low, less than $100 a month. Push Design CEO David Mosrie describes the advantages of hemp building construction:

> [Hemp is the] most effective and sustainable material available worldwide. The qualities it offers are beyond anything we get from typical materials, combining energy efficiency . . . strength, several hundred year wall lifespan, and the breathability and indoor air quality that is unsurpassed. It is an incredible combination, and a list of positive attributes we have never seen in any other material.[26]

Fab Tree Hab

Green building methods are being put to work in hemp homes, Earthships, and even in some skyscrapers. Yet no designs can be as green as the Fab Tree Hab, a home built inside a living tree. Plans for the home were developed at MIT by designers Mitchell Joachim, Javier Arbona, and Lara Greden.

Construction of a Fab Tree Hab begins with a scaffold, wood panels, and frames—all of which have been designed with a 3-D computer program. The scaffolds are placed around saplings. As the young trees grow, the scaffolds guide the formation of walls and a roof. Soy-based plastic windows are placed within the scaffolds of the Fab Tree Hab. The building is further shaped by a

The structure of this prototype Fab Tree Hab home incorporates living trees. To construct the house, designers placed scaffolds around young trees. As the trees grew, the scaffolds guided the formation of the walls and roof. The completed home is a living ecosystem, all made from natural resources.

process called pleaching, which is an ancient method of weaving together living tree branches as they grow to form archways and screen-like lattices. Although the process can take five years with fast-growing trees in a warm climate, it produces a single-family home that is not only good for the environment but also is part of the environment.

The Fab Tree Hab floor plan features a two-level house with a bathroom, living room, kitchen, dining area, and three bedrooms. The interior walls are finished with clay and straw panels that excel at blocking out moisture and keeping in warmth. The Fab Tree Hab is powered by solar and wind energy. It is designed to collect water on the rooftop and circulate it into the structure for human use. Gray water is drained into ponds where bacteria, fish, and plants remove the organic waste. The cleaned water can then be used to water the tree that provides the walls and roof of the Fab Tree Hab.

pleaching

An ancient method of weaving together living tree branches so they grow to form archways and screen-like lattices.

The designers of Fab Tree Habs envision a future where a home is started in a large nursery and then transplanted into a homeowner's building lot. The homes are expected to have a life span of around one hundred years. But the designers need to solve several problems before building a community of Fab Tree Habs. According to Joachim, "How do you insure a tree-based home? How do you find a carpenter that is also a botanist? How will a [municipal] planning board deal with a home that's always expanding? These are tough questions, but the benefit to the environment is huge."[27]

Free from Fossil Fuels

Although the Fab Tree Hab is still in the planning stage, green designers have found simpler ways to integrate live plants into buildings. Green walls are large vertical gardens attached to the exterior or interior of a building. The plant-filled walls replace large areas of plaster or brick. Green walls act as insulation to lower energy consumption by keeping a building cool in the summer and warm in the winter.

Green walls and living tree homes work with nature to provide shelter. Other designs incorporate garbage such as scrap tires or cans. Whatever the elements of a green building, the structures all have features in common. Green buildings save energy, they are carbon neutral, and they provide a vision of the world freed from fossil fuels.

CHAPTER FIVE

The Internet of Things

Tony Fadell is well known in the tech world as one of the designers of Apple's iPod music player. Years later he embarked on a new venture: redesigning the traditional household thermostat. The idea for the venture occurred while Fadell was building a high-tech vacation home in Northern California. He needed a thermostat to regulate the temperature of his house, but the standard ones were ugly, clunky, and dumb—meaning they could not be controlled remotely with a smartphone or computer. Fadell decided to design his own. Toward that end, he and a partner founded Nest Labs in 2010. The company designs and manufactures sleek, programmable Wi-Fi-enabled thermostats.

The Nest Learning Thermostat is designed to optimize heating and cooling of buildings to conserve energy. Users can program and control the thermostat using the Internet. The Nest features self-learning technology: it notes when residents arrive, leave, go to bed, and get up in the morning, and it adjusts the temperature accordingly. Users can tweak the temperature with a computer or phone app.

The Nest is one of hundreds of so-called smart devices on the market that are outfitted with Wi-Fi capabilities. Smart devices include smartphones, watches, coffeemakers, cameras, home weather monitors, kitchen appliances, fitness trackers, and even toys. The smart devices rely on sensors that measure and evaluate data.

Sensors and smart devices are increasingly referred to in the tech world as *things*. Futurists envision an interconnected web of sensors and smart devices that communicate with each other on a giant digital network called the Internet of Things (IoT). According to tech writer Daniel Burrus, "The Internet of Things revolves around increased machine-to-machine communication; it's built on cloud computing and networks of data-gathering sensors; it's mobile, virtual, and [allows] instantaneous connection."[28]

Google purchased Fadell's company for $3.2 billion in 2014. Tech writer Owen Poindexter explains the importance of the purchase: "Many hailed it as a sign of the arrival of Internet of Things. . . . Devices [like the Nest] are central to the Internet of Things—a hyper-connected environment in which all of our things become more responsive, dynamic, and . . . capable of chipping away at the excesses of our energy-intensive lifestyle."[29]

A Legion of Bots

The IoT is going to transform the way the modern world functions. By 2020 the number of connected devices and sensors on the IoT is expected to be between 26 billion and 100 billion. By that time anything that can be connected to the Internet will be connected. An interlinked web of Wi-Fi devices and sensors will make cities, buildings, and transportation networks extremely energy efficient. As tech journalist Bill Wasik describes it, "These connected objects will act more like a swarm of drones, a distributed legion of bots, far-flung and sometimes even hidden from view but nevertheless coordinated as if they were a single giant machine."[30]

sensor

An electronic object that detects, measures, and responds to a physical property such as heat, light, motion, pressure, or other environmental stimuli.

The IoT will create a smart world by linking major pieces of infrastructure, including streetlights, roads, bridges, utilities, airports, seaports, and factories. In addition to convenience and efficiency, smart devices will save energy and benefit the environment. As energy analyst Mauricio Chede writes, "Smart is the new green."[31]

The Smart House

Alex Hawkinson is already using the IoT to make his home smarter and greener. Hawkinson is a tech entrepreneur and the CEO of SmartThings, which develops apps, devices, and sensors to make homes smarter. Hawkinson's six-bedroom home on

The Nest thermostat (pictured) differs from regular programmable thermostats due to its self-learning technology. It notes the habits of a home's residents and adjusts the temperature accordingly. Moreover, it is Wi-Fi-enabled, so users can tweak it with a computer or phone app.

a 5-acre (2 ha) plot in Great Falls, Virginia, has over two hundred sensors that communicate with one another.

Everything from the garage door to the coffeemaker is connected to Hawkinson's SmartThings system. When he leaves his office, sensors in his smartphone automatically tell his home air conditioning system to power up so the house is cool when he arrives. In the winter, thermostats work with motion sensors to heat only occupied rooms. Moisture sensors in the lawn tell sprinklers to turn on when the grass is dry. The swimming pool heats up when Hawkinson lists a weekend barbeque on his digital calendar.

Smart Parking Meters

Sensors and digital devices can also be used on a large scale to solve parking problems. This is happening in San Francisco, a city with 380,000 cars and only 320,000 parking spaces. To make parking easier, in 2012 the city installed eighty-two hundred smart parking meters outfitted with wireless sensors. The sensors in the meters work with sensors embedded in the roadway to detect when a parking space is open. This information is relayed in real time to an app that drivers download onto their smartphones. The app can also be used with a credit card to pay for parking at the meter.

There are numerous benefits to smart parking, especially in a crowded city like San Francisco. Studies by the city show that smart meters reduced average parking search time by 43 percent, from eleven minutes down to six minutes. Likewise, city officials believe they have reduced the number of miles driven within the city by 30 percent. Fewer cars in search of parking means clearer roads, less wasted gas, and decreased air pollution. Other cities, including Los Angeles, are hoping to imitate San Francisco's success by instituting smart meter pilot programs.

The Internet of Energy

As the human population continues to grow, cities are going to need more than smarter parking meters to function. According to the United Nations, by 2050 more than 66 percent of the world's population will be living in cities, and 2.5 billion people will live in megacities with more than 10 million inhabitants. Researchers believe this will lead to the evolution of smart cities with features that include smart buildings, smart mobility, smart energy, smart information communication and technology, and smart governance. One consulting firm that does analysis and market research in this area predicts that about forty smart cities will exist globally by 2025. These cities will increasingly rely on renewable energy sources, with millions of rooftops holding wind turbines, solar panels, or other renewable energy devices. These small- and medium-sized energy sources will need to be coordinated with large power plants to provide electricity when and where it is needed. A smart energy grid based on the IoT will be at the heart of this system.

The Smart City of the Future

In the coming decades, cities will become smarter, cleaner, and more energy efficient due to the Internet of Things. Norwegian scientist Ovidiu Vermesan and tech innovator Peter Friess define smart cities this way:

> A smart city is defined as a city that monitors and integrates conditions of all of its critical infrastructures, including roads, bridges, tunnels, rail/subways, airports, seaports, communications, water, power, even major buildings. [The smart city will] better optimize its resources, plan its preventive maintenance activities, and monitor security aspects while maximizing services to its citizens. . . .
>
> In the long term Smart Cities vision, systems and structures will monitor their own conditions and carry out self-repair, as needed. The physical environment, air, water, and surrounding green spaces will be monitored in non-obtrusive ways for optimal quality, thus creating an enhanced living and working environment that is clean, efficient, and secure and that offers these advantages within the framework of the most effective use of all resources.

Ovidiu Vermesan and Peter Friess, eds., *Internet of Things—from Research and Innovation to Market Deployment.* Aalborg, Denmark: River, 2014, p. 43.

A smart grid will rely on sensors in power plants, power transmission lines, green power generators, and banks of computers to operate and manage the systems. Sensors will monitor power use, search for breakdowns, fix problems, and regulate electrical input from thousands of privately owned solar panels and wind turbines funneling excess power into the grid. A smart grid will also anticipate spikes in demand by analyzing environmental information such as weather forecasts and local conditions.

The grid will interact with every utility customer. Sensors in individual homes will communicate with the grid to report on electricity used by electric cars, appliances, heaters, air conditioners, and lighting systems. The Norwegian scientist Ovidiu Vermesan describes the system as an Internet of energy in which electrons flow in much the same way data now moves on the Internet: "The Smart Grid is . . . a kind of 'Internet' in which the energy packet is managed similarly to the data packet—across routers and gateways which can decide the best pathway for the [electricity] to reach its destination."[32]

With the Internet of energy, every home, office, and business will have a smart electric meter allowing users to monitor their power consumption on a minute-by-minute basis. People can then identify and eliminate energy-wasting devices. Smart meters will also interface with smartphones and personal computers to display the cost of electricity at any given moment. People will then be motivated to charge their electric cars and storage batteries at night, when prices are lower and excess power is produced.

The Internet of Vehicles

The smart grid will work in tandem with a city's smart transportation infrastructure. Smart cars, buses, trolleys, and trains will wirelessly connect with sensors in roads, bridges, traffic lights, and other systems. This will create an Internet of vehicles based on communications between vehicles and from vehicle to device, vehicle to infrastructure, and vehicle to grid.

The development of the Internet of vehicles is already under way. Driverless cars and buses, called autonomous vehicles (AVs), are being developed by tech companies such as Google and Apple, and by almost every carmaker. In 2010, for instance, a self-driving Audi drove the 12-mile (19 km) Hill Climb course to Colorado's Pikes Peak, successfully navigating the 156 turns along the steep mountain road. And in 2013 a Mercedes-Benz sedan navigated a 62-mile (100 km) journey through city streets in Germany without a driver.

autonomous

Acting independently; functioning without outside control.

Autonomous vehicles are more energy efficient because they accelerate smoothly, maintain steady speeds, and avoid harsh

This apartment building in San Jose, California, is equipped with solar panels and a green roof. Scientists predict that by 2025, at least forty smart cities featuring millions of similarly equipped buildings will be in existence.

braking—all of which reduces gas consumption. According to Dave McCreadie, Ford Motor's manager of electric vehicles: "If you have a fully autonomous car that talks to other cars and traffic signals, then it can drive more smoothly, much better than a human can, and there will be fuel economy benefits coming out of that."[33] According to a 2014 report by the Intelligent Transportation Society of America, an organization that promotes advanced transportation systems, AVs combined with the Internet of vehicles could reduce greenhouse gas emissions by 30 to 40 percent by 2025.

The Smart Road Ahead

A continuous information loop between autonomous vehicles, sensors, satellites, traffic control devices, and human observers will coordinate traffic to reduce energy consumption. The Internet of vehicles will allow AVs to link up with other cars driving a similar route. The vehicles will be able to travel in so-called flocks, close together at high speeds as one entity. This mode of travel is extremely efficient. There will be no traffic jams, and vehicles will not have to waste energy stopping and starting.

A smart highway system can be linked to smart rail and other public transportation systems. Rather than driving privately owned vehicles, travelers will plan their journeys based on any and all available means. With smart travel, the ideal way to get from point A to point B might involve a mix of autonomous cars, buses, trains, and vehicle sharing. However, most researchers do not see any such systems in place until around 2030. Specialized computers and software will be needed to coordinate the data from billions of moving parts, and safety has to be ensured.

Experts say a smart highway grid will reduce traffic fatalities by 80 percent, but digital systems can still cause problems. Hackers can tamper with cars that depend on software and wireless connections to steer, brake, and navigate. This was demonstrated in 2015 when two cybersecurity researchers remotely put a Jeep Cherokee into a ditch by hacking the vehicle's satellite-connected sound and entertainment system. Another team of cybersecurity experts took control of a Tesla Model S by hacking the car's entertainment system. Both companies installed patches to plug the security holes, but as massive wireless systems are put in place to control highways and other infrastructure, hacking will remain a threat.

Solar Roads

Smart cars might be even more energy efficient if they could drive on smart highways. This is the view of Scott and Julie Brusaw, cofounders of Solar Roadways. The Brusaws believe that smart roads might one day be constructed from millions of solar panels laid end to end. Their company, based in Idaho, has developed a pavement system that generates electricity and even melts snow and ice on contact. This feature frees cities from using energy-sucking snowplows, sanders, and dump trucks. The roadway solar panels also have numerous safety features. They contain built-in LED lights that flash to warn drivers of upcoming traffic or accidents. Additionally, the panels send information to road signs

A self-driving smart car developed by Google makes its way through the streets of Mountain View, California. These types of vehicles are more energy efficient than human-driven cars because they accelerate and brake smoothly and maintain consistent speeds. Some researchers believe that widespread use of the vehicles could greatly reduce greenhouse gas emissions.

that can display texts about downed tree limbs, construction projects, or other road hazards.

The idea of solar panels withstanding a daily pounding from cars, trucks, and weather might sound unlikely. But a Solar Roadways pilot project completed in 2012 has shown that solar highways work. Solar Roadways constructed a parking lot embedded with 108 solar panels in Sandpoint, Idaho. The panels were manufactured with typical rooftop solar panels encased in thick, bulletproof glass. Each panel can hold 250,000 pounds (113,400 kg)—equal to the weight of four fully-loaded semitrucks. The panels, which last twenty years and will not break or crack from accidents, have many smart features.

The panels in the Solar Roadways parking lot worked so well that the city of Sandpoint made plans in 2015 to install more of them at the airport, the Amtrak station, and on city roads and sidewalks. According to Scott Brusaw, if his company's solar panels were embedded in 20,000 square miles (51,800 sq km) of roads in the United States, they would generate three times more electricity than the nation uses annually. The next generation

From Theory to Application: The Internet of Things

The term *Internet of Things* was coined by technology pioneer Kevin Ashton in 1999 in reference to ways companies could link individual products together using the Internet. The idea received an added boost in 2005, when the International Telecommunications Union issued its yearly report, which it titled *The Internet of Things*. The report provided a blueprint for the IoT. In the report, the IoT was also called a sensing network since the application relies on a network of information-sensing objects that manage and control various systems. This equipment includes infrared sensors, GPS, laser scanners, and radio frequency identification, which identify and track objects including vehicles, consumer goods, and even people. The sensors are wirelessly joined on the Internet to form a giant intelligence network that can communicate and act without human intervention.

of roadway solar panels might even be able to transmit charges to electric vehicles as they roll down the road. The panels, however, remain expensive to produce, and currently many cities and states are reducing funds for highway repair and construction. Nonetheless, the company contends that a solar roadway project would pay for itself with the power generated and through less maintenance.

The online public seems to agree that solar roads are the next big thing. The Brusaws raised $1.9 million with a crowdfunding campaign, and the company's video *Solar Freakin' Roadways* went viral on social media, attracting over 13 million hits on YouTube.

An Interconnected Future

In the coming decades, the idea of an individual driver controlling a privately owned vehicle might be seen as a quaint relic of the past. According to futurist Gabe Klein, the decades ahead will see "widespread car sharing and driverless car rentals as well as fleets of self-driving cars . . . that could be summoned to homes and workplaces when needed. . . . There would be self-driving delivery vehicles and vehicles of various sizes designed for their roles, from small tricycles to large [autonomous] transit buses."[34] These vehicles will interface with an interconnected smart electric grid, smart roads, smart homes, and smartphones.

To many people, the Internet of Things may seem like something from a science fiction movie. As Poindexter notes, the IoT is where the Internet was in the early 1990s, "full of promise and potential but still a conceptual leap for most people."[35] And yet it is already moving forward; one day soon intelligent devices everywhere will be communicating and coordinating countless activities. In this new era, every machine, every home, every factory, and every city will work together as a single system to save energy while reducing the threat of climate change.

Source Notes

Introduction: New Ideas for Old Problems

1. Quoted in Christopher Adams and John Thornhill, "Gates to Double Investment in Renewable Energy Projects," *Financial Times*, June 25, 2015. www.ft.com.
2. Quoted in Adams and Thornhill, "Gates to Double Investment in Renewable Energy Projects."

Chapter One: Next-Generation Renewable Energy

3. José Luis Cordeiro, "Energy 2020: A Vision of the Future," Lifeboat Foundation, 2016. http://lifeboat.com.
4. Adam Boesel, Green Microgym, 2015. www.thegreenmicro gymbelmont.com.
5. Quoted in Rebecca Burns-Callander, "This Is the Next Generation of Renewable Energy Technologies," *Telegraph,* December 13, 2014. www.telegraph.co.uk.
6. Quoted in Australian Broadcasting Corporation News, "WA Wave Energy Project Turned On to Power Naval Base at Garden Island," February 17, 2015. www.abc.net.au.

Chapter Two: Battery Breakthroughs

7. Quoted in ScienceDaily, "New Design Points a Path to the 'Ultimate' Battery," October 29, 2015. www.sciencedaily.com.
8. Quoted in ScienceDaily, "Ultra-Fast Charging Batteries That Can Be 70% Recharged in Just Two Minutes," October 13, 2014. www.sciencedaily.com.
9. Quoted in James Morgan, "Hemp Fibres 'Better than Graphene,'" BBC News, August 13, 2014. www.bbc.com.
10. Quoted in John Lieberman, "Batteries That Run on Sugar Could Be in Gadgets in Just 3 Years," International Science Times, January 21, 2014. www.isciencetimes.com.

11. Quoted in Lieberman, "Batteries That Run on Sugar Could Be in Gadgets in Just 3 Years."

12. Quoted in Lakshmi Sandhana, "Scientists Create Weavable Li-Ion Fiber Battery Yarn," *Gizmag*, May 30, 2014. www.gizmag.com.

13. Quoted in Todd Woody, "Scientists Discover How to Generate Solar Power in the Dark," *Atlantic,* April 15, 2014. www.theatlantic.com.

14. Quoted in David L. Chandler, "A Molecular Approach to Solar Power," MIT News, April 13, 2014. http://news.mit.edu.

Chapter Three: Microbe Power

15. USDA, "President Obama's Climate Action Plan," October 2013. www.usda.gov.

16. Quoted in Tonya Maxwell, "With New Duke Natural Gas Plant, New Concerns," *Citizen-Times,* January 25, 2016. www.citizen-times.com.

17. Dairy Doing More, "How Do Digesters Work?," 2015. www.dairydoingmore.org.

18. Quoted in Dana Hull, "San Jose Biogas Facility Will Turn Food Waste into Energy," *San Jose Mercury News,* November 12, 2013. www.mercurynews.com.

19. Quoted in Charles Q. Choi, "Powerful Ideas: Beer Waste Makes Fuel," LiveScience, August 21, 2009. www.livescience.com.

20. Quoted in Martin LaMonica, "Bio-Energy Box Converts Beer Waste to Electricity," *IEEE Spectrum*, February 10, 2014. http://spectrum.ieee.org.

Chapter Four: Green Buildings

21. Quoted in Office of Waste Management, "Environmental Benefits of Recycling," University of Massachusetts, Amherst, 2006. www.umass.edu.

22. *ArchDaily* (blog)*,* "Can Cube/Archi Union Architects," October 27, 2010 www.archdaily.com.

23. Michael E. Reynolds, "Radically Sustainable Buildings," Earthship Biotechture, 2015. http://earthship.com.
24. Michael E. Reynolds, "Comfort in Any Climate," Earthship Biotechture, 2015. http://earthship.com.
25. Quoted in Nishat Awan, Tatjana Schneider, and Jeremy Till, *Spatial Agency: Other Ways of Doing Architecture.* New York: Routledge, 2011.
26. Quoted in Grant Banks, "The House Made of Hemp," *Gizmag,* November 30, 2010. www.gizmag.com.
27. Quoted in *Vancouver Sun,* "Grow Your Own Home: 'Fab Tree Hab,'" 2015. www.canada.com.

Chapter Five: The Internet of Things

28. Daniel Burrus, "The Internet of Things Is Far Bigger than Anyone Realizes," *Wired,* November 2014. www.wired.com.
29. Owen Poindexter, "The Internet of Things Will Thrive on Energy Efficiency," GovTech.com, July 28, 2014. www.govtech.com.
30. Bill Wasik, "In the Programmable World, All Our Objects Will Act As One," *Wired,* May 14, 2013. www.wired.com.
31. Mauricio Chede, "Smart Is the New Green in Latin America," Frost & Sullivan, August 23, 2013. www.frost.com.
32. Ovidiu Vermesan and Peter Friess, eds., *Internet of Things—from Research and Innovation to Market Deployment*. Aalborg, Denmark: River, 2014, p. 47.
33. Quoted in Ucilia Wang, "Are Self-Driving Vehicles Good for the Environment?," Ensia, August 17, 2015. http://ensia.com.
34. Quoted in Dan Weikel, "Pluses of Driverless Vehicles," *Los Angeles Times,* November 20, 2015, p. B8.
35. Poindexter, "The Internet of Things Will Thrive on Energy Efficiency."

For Further Research

Books

Lydia Bjornlund, *What Is the Future of Alternative Energy Cars?* San Diego: ReferencePoint, 2014.

Sylvia Engdahl, ed., *Energy Alternatives.* Farmington Hills, MI: Greenhaven, 2015.

Robert Green, *How Renewable Energy Is Changing Society.* San Diego: ReferencePoint, 2015.

Elizabeth Rusch, *The Next Wave: The Quest to Harness the Power of the Oceans.* New York: HMH, 2014.

Bryan Stone and Carmella Van Vleet, *Explore Electricity! With 25 Great Projects*. White River Junction, VT: Nomad, 2014.

Websites

Earthship (http://earthship.com). Earthships are extremely sustainable buildings made from old tires, earth, and other recycled materials. The company's website features photos of many homes and information about Earthships constructed all over the world, from New Mexico to New Zealand.

ExtremeTech (www.extremetech.com). This site covers the latest developments in technology in fields including computing, medical tech, gaming, space, and energy. The writers explain new developments in science in plain language and provide links to articles that cover similar topics.

Future Technology (www.alternative-energy-news.info/technology/future-energy). This website covers the latest developments in the alternative energy field, from hydrogen-powered trams to solar collectors that work at night. Articles cover next-generation concepts under development and those already in place around the world.

IEEE Spectrum (http://spectrum.ieee.org). The IEEE is the world's largest professional engineering and applied sciences organization. The *IEEE Spectrum* is the organization's magazine and website, which features blogs, podcasts, news stories, videos, and interactive infographics. Articles offer clear explanations of emerging concepts and developments in aerospace, computing, energy, gadgets, green tech, robotics, transportation, and more.

Internet of Things (www.wired.com/tag/internet-of-things). This blog, maintained by *Wired* magazine, covers the latest trends in embedded electronics, software, sensors, and network connectivity related to the Internet of Things. Articles cover an array of objects, from smart sprinklers and watches to medical devices and cars.

LiveScience (www.livescience.com/technology). The Tech section of this site covers the science behind the latest developments in technology, from robots and batteries to renewable energy and medcal tech.

Smart Highway (www.smarthighway.net). This website, hosted by Dutch designer Daan Roosegaarde, features descriptions and photos of innovative work, including glow-in-the-dark highway lighting and the Van Gogh bicycle path featuring thousands of glowing stones that charge by day and light the path by night.

Index

Note: Boldface page numbers indicate illustrations.

alternative energy research driver, 8–10
anaerobic digestion, 35
    See also biogas recovery systems
       (BRSs)
animal waste energy, 37–38
anode-respiring bacteria, 44
anodes, 24, 26
antimatter energy, 11, 19–22
Arbona, Javier, 56–58
Archi Union, 48
Arizona State University, 30–31
Ashton, Kevin, 68
autonomous, defined, 64
autonomous vehicles (AVs), 64–66, **67**
azobenzene, 32
Azura, 20

batteries
    biological (sugar), 28–30
    cigarette-butt, 29
    energy storage and release by, 12,
       23–24
    foldable, 30–31
    hemp super, 27–28
    potato, 33
    textile, 31–32
    thermal, 32–33
    titanium dioxide, 26–27
    See also lithium-ion (li-ion) batteries
Bear Republic Brewery, 44
beer waste, 42–44, **43**
Bengel, Wolfgang, 42
bicycling, 12–13, **13**, 14
bike desks, 14
Bio-Buses, 45
bioelectric systems, 43–44
biogas, 35, 36, 37
biogas recovery systems (BRSs)
    described, 35–36
    dog waste, 38
    EcoVolt reactors, 43–44
    in Europe, 42
    farms, 36–38
    municipal waste, 39–40

    sludge, 40–41
biological batteries (bio-batteries), 28–30
Blood, Steve, 14
Bloomington High School South
    (Indiana), 15
Boesel, Adam, 12–13, **13**
Bristol, England, 45
Brusaw, Julie, 66–68
Brusaw, Scott, 66–68
buildings, US energy consumption by, 47
buoy, defined, 19
buoy power, 18–19, 20
Burrus, Daniel, 59

calcify, defined, 55
Cambrian Innovation, 43–44
Can Cube building (Shanghai), 48–49
cannabis, 28
carbon dioxide (CO_2), 9, 35
carbon neutral, defined, 48
carbon neutral buildings. *See* sustainable
    architecture
Carnegie Wave Energy, 18–19
cars. *See* vehicles
cathodes, 24
cellulose acetate, 29
cement industry, 54
CETO wave-energy technology, 18–19
Chede, Mauricio, 60
Chen Xiaodong, 26–27
China, graphite mining, 26
cigarette-butt batteries, 29
cistern, defined, 50
cities
    growing population, 62
    heat islands, 54
    parking meters, 61–62
    See also smart cities
*Climate Action Plan—Strategy to Reduce
    Methane Emissions* (Obama), 35, 37
climate change, as driver of alternative
    energy research, 8–10
Clos du Bois winery, 44
coal, 8–9, 47
compressed air energy storage (CAES),
    16–17
concrete, 54

Cordeiro, José Luis, 11
corrosion, 17
costs
    antimatter, 21–22
    cigarette butts, 29
    natural gas power plants, 19
    Pavegen tiles, 15
    solar panels, 10
    wave energy, 17, 18–19, **18**
cows, 37
cybersecurity, 66

Dairy Doing More (website), 36
Department of Energy, 20
Dirac, Paul, 19–20
dog waste, 38

earth-sheltered homes, **49**, 49–52
Earthships, **49**, 49–52
EcoVolt reactors, 43–44
electric cars, 8, 23, 33–34
electricity generation
    by biogas, 37, 42–46
    by energy-plus houses, 47–48, 52–53,
        53
    by kinetic energy
        antimatter, 11, 19–22
        bicycling, 12–13, **13**, 14
        CAES, 16–17
        footsteps, 13–15
        waves, 17–19, **18**, 20
    off-peak excess used for CAES, 16–17
    percentage generated by coal and
        natural gas, 47
    by solar roads, 66–68
electrodes, 23–24, 26, 27
electrolytes, 24, 26, 30
energy consumption in US, 47
energy-plus houses, 47–48, 52–53, **53**
Environmental Protection Agency (EPA),
    35, 36, 38
enzymes, 29
eTURD, 38
Europe, 42, 55
exoelectrogens, defined, 44

Fab Tree Hab, 56–58, **57**
Fadell, Tony, 59
farms, 36–38
Field, Colin, 45
flocks of vehicles, 65–66
foldable batteries, 30–31

food waste
    amount of, in US, 39
    from beer, 42–44, **43**
    to fuel buses, 45
    treatment in Los Angeles County,
        40–41
fossil fuels, 8–9, 10
Friess, Peter, 63
Fudan University (Shanghai, China),
    31–32
futurist, defined, 62

garbage
    landfills, **37**
    municipal solid waste, 39–40, 45
gardens, 50
Gates, Bill, 9–10
geothermal wells, 52
Gilbert (Arizona) dog waste recovery, 38
graphene, 27–28, **31**
graphite, 26
gray water, 50, 57
Greden, Lara, 56–58
green buildings. See sustainable
    architecture
Green Microgym, 12–13, **13**
green roofs, **65**
green walls, 54, 58
Grey, Clare, 23
Grossman, Jeffrey, 32

Harvard University, 32
Hawkinson, Alex, 60–61
Heathrow Airport, 15
Hebrew University (Jerusalem, Israel), 33
hempcrete (hemcrete), 54–56
Hemp House, 55–56
hemp hurds, 54–56
hemp super batteries, 27–28
highways, smart, 65–68
HMAS Stirling naval base, Australia,
    18–19
hot springs, 52
hoverboards, 24, **25**
Howarth, Robert, 36
hurds, 54

India, 14
infrastructure, 15, 64–68
International Telecommunications Union,
    68
Internet of energy, 62–64

Internet of Things (IoT), 59, 68
Internet of vehicles, 64–68
ion, defined, 24
irrigation by pedal power, 14

Joachim, Mitchell, 56–58

Kemball-Cook, Laurence, 13–14, 15
kinetic, defined, 12
kinetic energy
  antimatter energy, 11, 19–22
  produced by human muscle, 11
    bicycling, 12–13, **13**, 14
    CAES, 16–17
    footsteps, 13–15
    waves, 17–19, **18**, 20
Klein, Gabe, 68–69

landfills, **37**
Large Hadron Collider (LHC), 21
Larvik energy-plus houses, 52–53, **53**
Levin, Julia, 40
LightSail, 17
lithium-ion (li-ion) batteries
  development of next generation, 23,
    25–27
  needed for electric cars, 34
  popularity of, 23
  problems with, 24, **25**
  woven into textiles, 31–32
London Olympics (2012), 14
Los Angeles, California, 40–41

machine-to-machine communication, 59
Massachusetts Institute of Technology,
  30, 32
matter, states of existence, 19
McCreadie, Dave, 65
methane
  BRS and, 36, 44
  from organic waste, 35
  as pollutant, 36
  as vehicle fuel, 39
microbes, 35, 44
microbial fuel cells, 43–46
Mitlin, David, 28
Miura, Koryo, 30
Miura fold, 30–31
Morro da Mineira neighborhood (Rio de
  Janeiro, Brazil) soccer field, 15, **16**
Mosrie, David, 56
municipal solid waste (MSW), 39–40, 45

Musk, Elon, 8

nanosheets, 27–28
nanotechnology, 26–27
nanotubes, 26, **27**
Nanyang Technology University (NTU,
  Singapore), 25–27
natural gas consumption, 47
Nest Labs, 59, 60
Nest Learning Thermostats, 59, **61**
Northwest Energy Innovations, 20

Obama, Barack, 35, 37
off-the-grid homes, 8
oil, 8–9
Olympic Park (London, England), 14
organic waste, 35
  See also specific types
origami batteries, 30–31
Ottaviano, Michael, 19

Pacific Gas & Electric (PG&E), 40, 41
parking meters, 61–62
particle colliders, 21
Pavegen, 13–15
Pedal Power, **13**, 14
photoswitching, 32–33
plants, waste from roots of, 45–46
pleaching, 56–57, 58
PNC Plaza Tower (Pittsburgh,
  Pennsylvania), 51
Poindexter, Owen, 60, 69
pollution
  carbon dioxide (CO_2), 9, 35
  graphene, 27–28
  graphite, 26
  methane, 36
  reductions in smart cities, 65
"Poo Bus," 45
potato batteries, 33
Powerwall, 8, 10
power plants, off-peak excess energy
  production, 16–17
Push Design, 55–56

rainwater harvesting, 49, 51
Rapoport, Benjamin I., 30
recycled materials for building, 48–52,
  49, 56
renewable energy technologies driver,
  8–10
Research Centre on Zero Emission

Buildings (Norway), 52–53, **53**
Reynolds, Michael E., **49**, 49–52
Rio de Janeiro, Brazil, 15, **16**
roads, solar, 66–68

San Francisco (California) dog waste
  recovery, 38
San Francisco (California) parking meters,
  61–62
San Jose, California, 39–40
scrap tires, **49**, 49–52
self-learning technology, 59–60, **61**
sensors, 59, 60–62, 63–64
Seoul National University (South Korea),
  29
Silver, Matthew, 44
skyscrapers, 51
sludge, **40**, 40–41
smart cities, **65**
  defined, 63
  energy grids in, 62–64
  number predicted, 62
  transportation infrastructure, 64–68
smart devices
  in homes, 59, 60–61, **61**
  parking meters, 61–62
SolarCity, 8
solar energy
  chimneys, 51
  costs, 10
  examples of, 8, **9**
  panels, **9**, **65**
    current cost, 10
    on Earthships, 50
    on Larvik energy-plus home, 52,
      53, **53**
    roads, 66–68
    on smart city buildings, 62–63, **65**
  photoswitching molecules and, 32–33
  roads, 66–68
  storage of, 8
Solar Freakin' Roadways (video), 68
Solar Roadways, 66–68
solar storage batteries (SSBs), 8
Sony, 23
soy-based plastic, 56
steel, recycled, 48, 53
sugar batteries, 28–30
supercapacitors (supercaps), 27–28, **31**
sustainable architecture
  carbon-neutral buildings, 47
  energy-plus houses, 47–48, 52–53, **53**

Fab Tree Hab, 56–58, **57**
goal of, 47
green walls, 54, 58
hemp buildings, 54–56
increase in construction of, 47
Internet of Things and, 59–61
recycled building materials used,
  48–52, **49**, 56
sustainable construction techniques,
  53–56
zero-energy buildings, **49**, 49–52

Tesla Motors, 8, 34
textile batteries, 31–32
thermal batteries, 32–33
thermostats, programmable Wi-Fi-
  enabled, 59, **61**
titanium dioxide batteries, 26–27
Toronto dog waste recovery, 38
tree-based homes, 56–58, **57**

University of Hawaii, 20
urban heat islands, 54
US Navy Wave Energy Test Site, 20

vehicles
  biogas as fuel for, 39, 45
  electric, 8, 23, 33–34
  methane as fuel for, 39
  sharing, 68–69
  in smart cities, 64–66
  US energy consumption by, 47
Vermesan, Ovidiu, 63, 64
vertical gardens, 54, 58
Virginia Tech, 29

Wageningen University (Netherlands),
  45–46
Wasik, Bill, 60
wastewater, energy from, 43–44
wastewater treatment facilities, 41
wave energy, 17–19, **18**, 20
Wei Wang, 32
Wi-Fi, 59, 60
Wiley, Andrew, **13**

yard waste, 39

zero-energy buildings (ZEBs), **49**, 49–52
Zero Waste Energy Development
  (ZWED), 39–40
Zhang, Y.H. Percival, 29, 30

Picture Credits

About the Author

Stuart A. Kallen is the author of more than 350 nonfiction books for children and young adults. He has written on topics ranging from the theory of relativity to the art of electronic dance music. In addition, Kallen has written award-winning children's videos and television scripts. In his spare time he is a singer, songwriter, and guitarist in San Diego.